AVOIDING THE JUDAS COMPLEX

by
VIRGIL HURLEY

Black Forest Press
San Diego, California
September, 2001
First Edition

AVOIDING THE JUDAS COMPLEX

by
VIRGIL HURLEY

PUBLISHED IN THE UNITED STATES OF AMERICA
BY
BLACK FOREST PRESS
P.O.Box 6342
Chula Vista, CA 91909-6342

Dedicated To:

Darla, Robyn, Lori and Debbie:
Bound by marriage and by Christ's Love.

All scripture references are from the New International Version.

Printed in the United States of America
Library of Congress
Cataloging-in-Publication

ISBN: 1-58275-066-1

Table of Contents

INTRODUCTION

Extrapolate the questions, doubts and disappointments all Twelve disciples experienced, let them go unresolved because they unacceptably contradicted previous convictions one man wouldn't surrender—and there you have Judas Iscariot. If we take all their misunderstandings, limitations and political aspirations—and deprive them of trust and love, a Judas is inevitable. Meeting Jesus of Nazareth, a Judas is inevitable!

It isn't easy to understand Judas; or without peril to try. He has been unsparingly denounced, even by unbelievers. But such an horrendous disaffection couldn't occur in a vacuum. From Judas' viewpoint, he had at the time what seemed logical reasons for his decision. From disapproval, to disaffection, to alienation, to final betrayal he went, confident of his aptitude and of Christ's ineptitude. That he later regretted his action is beside the point. *At the time,* he felt justified in betraying Jesus. I've tried to show this in Parts I-III by putting Judas in the Hinnom Valley the early morning after the betrayal, explaining to posterity why he grew disenchanted with the rabbi he had once loved.

Only in the after-experience of the arrest and trial did he rethink his actions—and these I have tried to stress in the Retrospects where provided. We obviously can't be certain of what he said, but the Retrospects accurately coincide with spiritual truth that would have made them possible, even for someone like Judas. He was an intelligent man, after all. He certainly knew at the end that he had bungled his privilege. He had thought his life couldn't get worse if he stopped believing in Jesus, then found it could—and **did!**

Part IV stresses several of the principles Judas overlooked as he ignored a spiritual king in his fixation on a political kingdom. He wasn't alone of the Twelve in ignoring them, but he was alone of the Twelve in not being amenable to correction!

A study of Judas is important to us because he represents a danger most Christians ignore or deny: discipleship experience offers no guarantee against ultimate discipleship failure. Satan loves to delude the Christian community into thinking we have nothing in common with Judas, or that he has nothing to teach us. But the Judas Complex lurks in everyone, including believers, who insist on filtering divine truth through personal perspectives and experiences. As I wrote in my book, *Face To Face With Jesus*, the Judas Complex often has a subtle, equally deadly impact on Christians: it reduces or eliminates absolute trust in Christ, the lack of which keeps disciples from developing into the powerhouse believers he demands.

Satan encourages us to turn every unanswered prayer into doubt and every unanswered doubt into skepticism—because he knows that cynicism towards God always follows! *And he succeeds more often than we want to admit because we **are** ignorant of his devices!* When we abandon discipleship out of pique or disagreement, we embrace the Judas Complex. When we withhold obedience until we understand more clearly, we embrace the Judas Complex. When we question God's care for us, we embrace the Judas Complex. His Complex is most emphatic, not only in what it has made us, but in what it has kept us from becoming through Christ's presence. Indeed, the Judas Complex is always dormant or alive...in skeptics and in believers. Never think otherwise. Denying it's threat offers Satan an opportunity to intrude it just when we think we're free of it.

PART I

RECRUITMENT

ATTRACTION

Drawn by the charismatic Baptizer, I joined a host at the Jordan. Roused and captivated by the preaching of that engaging, yet menacing prophet, I welcomed his messianic emphasis and tolerated his calls for repentance. We all needed to become more religious, including myself; it would bring God's favor on our political efforts. We all needed to be less materialistic, myself included; I had become fond of my prosperous lifestyle.

I liked John's iron-mind intimidation of the arrogant. Only repentance would suffice, he shouted at those expecting privileges based on association with Abraham. My only dissatisfaction came from his response to Roman soldiers. When they asked, "what should we do?", I felt he should have thundered, "Do? You monsters? Why, go to Hell!" But no, he simply ordered them to stop abusing our people, then willingly baptized those professing a change of heart. Not what my compatriots wanted to hear!

When fame raised expectations among common people that he might be Messiah, an inexplicable softness eclipsed his usual adamant manner. He quietly explained that he baptized only with water while the Coming One would baptize with the Holy Spirit. I had no idea what that meant or who might be more powerful than John; he was easily the most formidable personality I had ever seen. Though he performed no miracles, who possibly could be more respected by so many—and feared by so many more?

I gladly complied with John's insistence on baptism, becoming his disciple.

One day, about six months after he began preaching, a startling change occurred in John. People stood in line for baptism, walked into the water, heard a few words from him, said a few in return, turned, were immersed against the current, then exited the river into the desert sun.

The long line moved forward person by person to receive his ministration. Suddenly, as one man stood before him, the Baptist became deferential! The very same man who feared no one, rebuked everyone, called the religious leaders snakes and secular rulers condemned sinners, the very same John turned respectful and submissive! I heard his words float across the water: "I need to be baptized by you, and do you come to me?" The religious iconoclast had never hinted at such words! Yet, like clay in the potter's hand, he yielded when the man insisted.

We expected the candidate, like everyone else, to instantly exit the waters; but he remained in place while John cocked his head, as if hearing an otherwise soundless voice, then lifted his eyes skyward to watch an otherwise invisible sight. After a few minutes the man shook John's hand, turned and left the water and the area. We watched him depart, then turned back to John—where a glow shone in his usually-angry face!

Who was that man to so completely captivate our immovable John the Baptist?

About two months later, greater crowds still flocked to the hermit preacher. One morning, while everyone breakfasted, awaiting John's sermons, I saw a stranger fording the Jordan upstream from the baptismal site. John had also seen him. His gaze became specific, then fixed. Then, completely unlike him, the seated John rose and walked to greet the man.

As they met and exchanged kisses—John didn't offer that gratuity to anyone—he appeared mesmerized by the stranger's presence. As the man went his way, John shook himself free from whatever spell had seized him, hurriedly called some of his disciples, pointed at the departing figure and breathtakingly exclaimed: "Look, the lamb of God who takes away the sin of the world!"

Again, totally unlike him, he offered an explanation for his unusual behavior. He had heard and seen the strangest things after the man's baptism, he told us—he could hardly keep the news quiet at the time, and now felt free to share it— the Holy Spirit descended on the man: an all-important bequest because God had promised John it would happen only for the Messiah. Then God's booming approval confirmed the man's identity!

Acquainted with him as John was—they were cousins on their mothers' side— John originally couldn't understand why he had presented himself for baptism. He, of all the people John knew, didn't fit the profile! With the baptism completed, however, John instantly understood: no wonder Jesus of

Nazareth didn't need baptism—he was the Son of God!   The baptism had been for John's instruction, not his cousin's forgiveness!

So that's what John saw weeks ago!, I ruminated. *That's why he stood staring into the sky, then at the man when he left the Jordan. Jesus of Nazareth: if he is greater than John, and John said he is, **who** is he? He surely deserves my attention!*

PART II

DISENCHANTMENT

DISAVOWAL OF WEALTH

From the time he scattered the coins of temple money-changers, I questioned teacher's financial values and fiscal integrity. I didn't realize he would systematically undermine the prosperity-for-obedience teachings sanctified by generations of rabbis. Had I followed my instincts, not my idealism, I would have stalked out with the authorities, saving myself the despair now haunting me.

I soon discovered that I alone of the disciples understood the shekel's value; to a man the rest shared rabbi's naivete. To justify their penury, they perhaps thought others should have less. Or perhaps they mistakenly imported village simplicity to the money-focused complexity of city life.

Consistent with the temple cleansing, Jesus insisted that both sets of brothers abandon their nets to follow him. How did he propose to care for their families while he took their men away, who knew where, to return to them, who knew when?

Then came his equally enigmatic call to Levi, who shared my business background, without my financial acumen. At rabbi's behest he surrendered his business—just turned it over to another. And, to celebrate the change from first-rate banker to mendicant, Levi spent money he no longer had to thank rabbi for disenfranchising him.

Wouldn't it have been more business-like to grant him a share in the duty station, providing us a cash reserve for emergency use? Couldn't his continued contacts assure the financial support of many like him, refueling resources constantly diminished by a demanding ministry?

However, at the time, the fact that he called Levi raised my hopes. If rabbi wanted men with monetary expertise, I certainly qualified. When, a few months later he rewarded my aspirations by incorporating me into the Twelve, euphoria suffused me! I at first thought he chose me *for* my business background; hadn't he allowed my appointment as Treasurer? Since he had no experience in commerce—and knew the rest uncritically accepted his opinions, he needed my genius to offer informed counsel, to challenge his inexperience and clarify his teachings, especially in reference to revenues. The balance my erudition brought would probe the potential or see the dangers in his policies and procedures.

Indeed, while I thought inclusion in his inner group would silence my doubts—wouldn't he discuss issues with the Twelve, seeking consensus before taking a position sure to create controversy, accepting accountability to us?—the opposite occurred. It soon became evident that he intended to sculpt us in his image, not suffer any mutual sculpturing by striking his iron against ours.

As a minor example of how he offended me with his every teaching about money—it would get much more flagrant—teacher loved to eat on fast days. He didn't seem to realize that, at the very least, observing our culture's fasts reduced food costs and my worry about providing the next meal. Rabbi could have shown me respect me in their observance.

He also demanded that we give, not only our inner, but our outer coat to a litigant. He didn't appreciate the time and effort needed to make our garments. On another occasion I heard him say we should give up what wealth we had to secure eternal habitations, implying that God intended us to sacrifice, not enjoy, the material benefits he granted. No rational Jew accepted that!

Could he really believe you created wealth by distributing it? Why not let the rich keep their resources, encourage them to gain more, then give more to the poor? That way everybody had something, and the truly deserving, industrious and gifted had most. That preserved our generations-old tradition!

Instead, rabbi constantly harped on our need to trust God for daily provisions. I knew the slender margin between financial survival and disaster, and how close to catastrophe we always lived. Living by faith wouldn't buy lunch in the bazaar, when everyone of those men expected to eat and me to feed them!

I had to admit, however: he never worried! When I voiced concerns for our fiscal health, or mentioned that we hardly had enough for ourselves when people begged our help, he counseled me to "trust God; he will provide." I got heartily sick of hearing it and of living hand to mouth, rescued at the last minute by donations from a rich man's servant, or by women, or by people little better off than we sharing from their poverty. That seemed my strongest argument; if we had several financial giants bolstering us, we wouldn't totter constantly at the financial abyss.

The other men seemed resigned to it, even to glorying in the providential offerings from unknown sources, but it had no appeal for me. It especially exasperated me that Levi could so uncritically embrace that haphazard lifestyle.

Rabbi also loved to compare our needs to birds and plants; as if no difference existed between living creatures feeding off a luxuriant earth and laborers impoverished by impious landlords who paid too little and a foreign government that took too much! I often thought rabbi would be better served to *feed* people than assure them they *could be* fed!

I especially resented his demand that we store up treasure in heaven, not on earth. I thought, *Rabbi, thieves may break in and steal your treasure, but isn't it better to have something thieves want? Wouldn't there be a lot less worrying about tomorrow if we had more money today?*

Personally, I felt comfortable in the company of wealthy people. And, while the disciples often belittled my worries, none of them refused invitations to their feasts. That offered me another proof of money's value.

I *never* understood why rabbi so uniformly deprecated the gifts of wealth and exalted the gifts of poverty. After hearing him scorch the Sanhedrin a few days ago, we disciples stood apart talking about his blistering attack, glancing at him, then at the crowd which had withdrawn. Supercharged by his assault, and oblivious of their departure, he studied intently as people walked through the temple, past the Treasury.

Something suddenly animated him and he stood, a big smile creasing his face, those mysterious eyes glistening! We came when he motioned us over and looked in the direction he pointed. We saw the well-dressed wealthy casting many coins that rattled through trumpet shapes into boxes below. But he hadn't been attracted by that, he said. No, as he had a maddening habit of doing, he noticed an old woman dressed in rags! When he explained why, I could only shake my head in disgust: *because she gave all she had!*

He noticed a widow who gave nearly nothing, not the rich who gave much! Though they paid the bills for her place of worship. A thousand like her couldn't keep *one* of those thirteen receptacles functioning, while a few of them kept them *all* flourishing. To say nothing of giving the expensive jewels with which the rich embroidered the temple!

Had he ever considered that only Herod's lavish expenditures made our magnificent temple possible? Would he have preferred the "good old days," when our people camped in the wilderness before the portable tabernacle? Or the hopelessly outclassed structure Zerubbabel built? Didn't he realize that people came from all points of the Roman compass to visit Jerusalem and the temple? Wealth made that possible.

Had envy overcome rabbi? Since he had little, did he instinctively mistrust those with much? Since he had only faith in God, did he automatically consign others to materialism? Since he never had the responsibility of family and children, did he irrationally show no concern for worried fathers and mothers? Since he had become a holy man living off the productivity of others, would he unreasonably condemn the very generosity that made him possible?

To me, seeking both God's kingdom *and* wealth summarized our national existence, expressed in the teachings of generations. One's interest could be in Heaven through one's wealth. Instead, he repeatedly warned about the dangers money posed—*dangers,* not *possibilities*—I noticed he always said! He preferred poverty to wealth because wealth could be abused? As if poverty couldn't! As if poor people didn't use their poverty as an excuse to steal! As if all the rich were selfish tyrants, and all the poor selfless pastors! As if virtue existed in abandoning all that one's industry, skill and thrift gained!

I heard this mantra many times, but two glaring instances in his later ministry hardened my opposition to him. The first occurred when a man interrupted teacher to request mediation in an estate dispute. When given the opportunity to show interest in daily life, and speak to problems people faced, he turned instead to issues of greed and covetousness. As if wanting justice in dividing one's inheritance had no relevance. The selfish brother, not the one merely seeking justice, needed teacher's lecture about the rich man's worries.

What was better to worry about?, I wondered: *escaping the poverty that enslaved or keeping the possessions that lib-*

erated? Of course, it took effort and sometimes demanded anxiety to oversee one's investments, but better to worry about keeping them than to forlornly wish for them! Plenty of people would accept the burdens to enjoy the privilege! Especially I, having neither the burden nor the privilege, but only a treasury swamped by causes rabbi never failed to support.

Then came his glaring mistreatment of the young ruler, a man I considered the epitome of righteousness. I mentally lectured, *rabbi, finally here's a man with no hidden agenda, as the Pharisees often have, putting you on edge, making you carefully choose your words, leading to exasperating digressions. He wants answers for his soul. He's even admitting your superiority to Moses.*

The man's request obviously resonated to rabbi's depths. A special fondness crossed his face. Would he finally express appreciation of a wealthy man? More hopefully and pointedly, would he enlist him as a disciple?

Not ever! He adamantly demanded surrender of the man's wealth!

I caught an expletive before it left my mouth, but I cursed within, *rabbi, why not let him follow as a rich man? Since you invited him, why plunder him first? Here's as good a man as I've met, wanting nothing more than all Israelites seek! Why attack his wealth? How does that relate to eternal life? Why does being poor assure, and being rich endanger the eternal life we all seek?*

Infuriated, I wondered how an itinerant teacher and his slovenly disciples could so needlessly offend a man with such potential. Or why rabbi constantly recruited those who could do nothing for him and continually affronted those who could do much!

Couldn't he at least have said to him, "Look, I'll make you my chief supporter. With your money backing my ministry, everything is possible; think what we can do! You can earn your place in my kingdom by supporting its causes."

If rabbi envisioned a kingdom, and would soon establish it, didn't he need deep pockets to bankroll the revolution, equip and support armies in the field and to make political, business and religious contacts?   Didn't the ruler own free-flowing wealth, contacts into an almost-untouched social stratum and a wild enthusiasm rare in his class? *More* of everything the man possessed existed, and it could have been ours, and I could have been in charge of it!

But no, teacher turned the ruler's quest into an *attack* on him, hopelessly complicating his call, adding conditions sure to offend him, making his obedience impossible! While we disciples envied the man's wealth, Jesus pitied his spiritual poverty, again imposing the old rule that affluence eliminated, not created religious faith! We thought he had so much potential because of his capital while rabbi figured him hopelessly shackled by it!

We couldn't believe he would let such a promising disciple leave; indeed, we couldn't believe he would make such demands on him! I wanted to shout, *rabbi, go after him. Make an exception! Think of our needs! Think what he can do for you. In a few weeks we'll be in Jerusalem!*

Instead...as a welcome bank account stalked off, teacher sadly shook his head and spoke plaintively, almost wistfully...how hard for a rich man to be saved!

Before I knew it, my exasperation exploded: "But rabbi, why is it always wrong to be rich?" Thankfully, after me others followed with questions that showed our common disenchantment with his values. Nonetheless, without explaining himself or answering our questions, he flatly and unequivocally warned us against trusting possessions.

"Then who can be saved?" Peter finally expostulated, even he growing weary of rabbi's disaffection with everything in our heritage. In return, rabbi meaninglessly replied about human inability and God's capability. As if we didn't know both! As if we didn't have the temple as God's reminder that only he could forgive sins.

Disavowing that man obliterated my faith in Jesus of Nazareth. *If he can't use him,* I said to myself, *he can't use me, and I have no use for him!* I knew he had to be stopped. I had to reach an understanding with the authorities!

It occurred to me even then, of course, that he occasionally expressed a positive interest in finances. He saw the need of the half-shekel for temple maintenance and applauded the dishonest steward's shrewdness in providing for his future. How strange that rabbi, with his exceptional integrity, actually applauded the steward's deceit. I never heard him refer to wealth without saying something revolutionary, but I never imagined he would applaud the dishonesty he always denounced!

On that same occasion he declared that money *could* secure one's eternal habitation. *Finally,* I exulted at the time, *exactly what our teachers have always said: wealth can be the sign of Heaven's favor and the means by which Heaven's favor can be extended*!

Why then contradict that clear teaching with equally strong, but opposing views? I couldn't understand the man!

Above all, while irrevocably hostile to opulence, rabbi said that his kingdom resembled hidden treasure and a great pearl! That being true, he himself established a relationship between money and the religious life. Why not value money then, since the kingdom is a treasure; and gems, since the kingdom is a pearl?

He certainly valued money when he considered the unfortunates. It was always, "Judas, give them a gift from our store." He refused payment for his miracles, though all would have gladly given something—and many gratefully much—but ordered me to help the poor. I always thought, *aren't we poor, teacher? Don't we live hand to mouth every day, never knowing where our daily bread will be baked*?

Yet, with the rich man, who would have financed any project rabbi advocated, including those "poor" he loved, he insisted he sell all he had. Why didn't he tell that to the women? Where would he have received support then? Is that why he didn't demand it of them? Perhaps...if he had shown more business acumen in his teachings about property, he could have built substantial undergirding for a settled ministry instead of being a wandering hermit on the dole!

Pharisees vocally scoffed at his views, as did I silently, not wanting to raise suspicions, but glad for their interposition, for rabbi's consistent preaching irritated nearly everyone. Like myself, they appreciated the way wealth marked them as God's favorites, eliminated so many worries and helped them ameliorate poverty. Rabbi unfairly denounced them as mere lovers of money instead of appreciative of money and the good it could achieve.

I couldn't deny that some, like Zacchaeus, agreed with rabbi and unconditionally surrendered their fortunes.

Zacchaeus even volunteered his! *But think, rabbi,* I stormed within, *since Zacchaeus shows such altruism, and you claim to represent Israel, why not encourage him to share his stolen wealth with the Twelve as repayment to our nation? Why not make that a condition of his discipleship?*

What strange magnetism he possessed to motivate the surrender of assets, station and security to vagabond the country with him! They should have learned from me: I fell prey to it at first, but the experience cured me!

Perhaps rabbi never thought it an inconsistency, but I felt that his personal unconcern for financial security rendered him insensitive to other peoples' economic problems, seen most egregiously in his destruction of the Gadarene pigs. That seemed a graceless response to their previous kindness to the man. They hadn't caused his condition, *had* made every effort to restrain him for his own good, then drove him away only when he became a threat to them! Why ruin their economy? Why heartlessly plunder a business that kept people living marginally just to prove he could drive them into indigence? Did religious conflict between God and Satan have to harm innocent people? Was it any wonder the Gadarenes had him leave? If someone came to my town, and first thing destroyed my livelihood, I would consider him a threat, not a benefactor.

Actually, if I understood correctly, rabbi violated their right of protection for private property, and of reimbursement if lost through another's negligence. Yet he made no offer to reimburse the people, and they didn't ask any—which was just as well since we could never have paid.

When, this past week, rabbi spoke of the destruction of Jerusalem, I **KNEW** my arrangement with the Sanhedrin was right. He plainly and brutally told of the coming obliteration of our city and culture! How could he so heartlessly predict our national demise? And...forecasting the worst of all disasters, warn that the very temple that housed God's Name and offered forgiveness of sin would be torn down block by block until it disappeared!

No one listening could have misunderstood: he had no appreciation of the wealth that built our nation's greatest city and our religion's most imposing edifice, in both of which countless millions had been invested! In a society where money was scarce, teacher considered it irrelevant. So I came to consider him an irrelevance!

RETROSPECT

Now I wonder: could rabbi have been right all along? After all, how oppressively the Sanhedrin's money weighed as I hid it on my person this week, afraid the others might see and wonder, and raise embarrassing questions that could expose me! And, when I confronted the leaders, I threw away the money I got for betraying him! *Threw it away!* Maybe he understood what I've just begun to feel: anyone who identifies contentment with prosperity faces ultimate embarrassment! For when circumstances change drastically enough, possessions mean *nothing at all*!

Maybe I've made the greedy person's mistake of claiming I wanted wealth for philanthropies when I really wanted it for egotism! If so, would I ever find satisfaction except in further acquisition? Would I succeed in *getting* more, only to feel myself a failure for not having acquired much more?

Then again, maybe possessions don't pose a threat if we don't trust them to provide our personal identity—as I have. Maybe rabbi was saying that the *love* of money renders its sacrifice necessary before we can love God. That could explain his command to the young ruler, for he imposed it on no one else, not even on Levi and Zacchaeus! Maybe the man placed his security and personal worth in his substance. So long as he maintained that focus, even I can now see that he couldn't love God, because God demands *priority*! For rabbi to accept the man purely *because* of his wealth would have insulted God. And since it was as natural for the ruler to trust his affluence as for the Romans to be arrogant, rabbi demanded he crucify that hubris instantly!

I'm also beginning to wonder if loving wealth doesn't *create* insurmountable obstacles to the spiritual life; if seeking it doesn't *imperil* the soul; if continuing to trust it doesn't *damn* the soul? For how can that person ever really be a disinterested benefactor? Won't his hope for reward determine the extent of his generosity: value received for value given? Surely all of our holy books, and all the rabbis, defy that person's entrance into God's presence.

Maybe I can now admit something else I previously denied: by putting God first, as Zacchaeus did, I *could* give away all I

had and live contentedly without; **rabbi did**. God *would*
provide and, by providing, prove himself the source of my
identity and esteem! For can't I now say that God provided for
us — until I inexcusably interfered by delivering teacher to
those Sanhedrin monsters! If only I had learned in time!

I admit that my pervasive, prolonged fondness of treasure
became an obsession, making the Sanhedrin's offer irresistible!
By considering myself a success only as I possessed wealth,
and rabbi a failure because he never would, I contemptuously
arranged his arrest since it brought me *some* of what I wanted
in *abundance*. Yet, having it, I abhorred it. Could I have
imagined that a year ago? The last few hours have abolished
my life-long values!

I can only mockingly laugh at another stupidity: I regretted
the money Mary "wasted" on Jesus, yet I wasted the money I
received for betraying him. I wanted to gain financially by my
association with rabbi — and hated his every refusal to honor
me. Yet, when I finally succeeded, I despised and abandoned
it! The inconsistency flogs my mind!

Now I admit my most glaring mistake: since what I once
considered indispensable proved expendable, I have embraced
deceit as truth! If, after having the reward, with no demand to
surrender it, I willingly threw it away because I couldn't justify
the behavior that earned it, it wasn't worth having at all, especially as my life's goal! That is the most scandalous evidence
of my failure: I left scattered over the floor at Caiaphas' palace
what belonged to me as fairly earned. Everyone's life-goal
comes to an end, but when it does, shouldn't we *value* what
we've lived by, not *despise* it? Shouldn't we extol its usefulness, not damn its irrelevance?

In the end, *I* paid for rabbi's arrest! The Sanhedrin got what
they wanted, perhaps rabbi got what he determined, but I got
nothing!!...oh, I got something, I ruefully admit...this determination to **end my life!**, but that only proves the fool I've been!

If I've failed as a disciple of Jesus of Nazareth, let me
succeed in challenging future generations: don't *love* money. It
has no use when death comes, so don't covet it while you live!
That preposterous lust led me to theft, which I now regret;
and to betrayal, which I now renounce!

REFUSAL TO ACCEPT PUBLIC ACCLAIM

The leaders of my generation so combatively disputed Messiah's coming that many replaced speculation with fatalism: wait patiently for God because he's faithful, they exclaimed! Our repentance wouldn't hasten Messiah's coming a day sooner than God planned, or delay it an hour later than God determined. Fatalism offended my activism, however; it stifled human initiative. Informed watchmen needed to discover potential claimants, then compare their giftedness with current needs.

Motivated by my convictions, I first found John, then Jesus. Abandoning John because he admitted he wasn't the Messiah, to follow the Jesus of Nazareth John said was, I eventually refused both. And, as the Baptist's disciples criticized rabbi for stealing publicity rightfully John's, I criticized him for refusing renown rightly his. With truculent persistence he dissented; with helpless persistence we begged him to reconsider. Our disparate views could no more merge than parallel Jerusalem streets.

He began his ministry with a prodigiously public cleansing of the temple and ended it with a prodigiously public entry into Jerusalem. But for three years in between imposed silence on his presence in Israel. It became an increasingly irritating point of contention!

I should have learned from one of the initial events in his first tour of Galilee. Mildly disconcerting as it was at the time, I excused it as an aberrant response. The spotted, emaciated leper instantly had new flesh when rabbi touched him—then strictly ordered privacy. I took silent exception! *If you want to become famous in Israel and be known as the great healer of our nation's wounds, rabbi, why perform such prodigies, then demand silence?*

As time passed I kept pondering his every denial. *Was it just reverse psychology,* I wondered, *intentionally creating as-*

tonishment, then ordering their response muffled, knowing people couldn't obey? If he didn't want to amaze people, why make himself a sensation? After all, rabbi got nothing for his prohibitions but increased fame, acclaim and wilder conjecture about his identity.

The constant thrill of being with him and hearing so many accolades encouraged our confidence, but had no effect on his denials. Like Essenes in their devotions, rabbi sought isolation as a means of public influence! He didn't establish the kingdom his every teaching and miracle forecast at hand. He instead sacrificed public esteem to retain a misplaced need of seclusion.

At first only random, indistinct and unsettling objections— apparent contradictions of what I had previously seen in the temple cleansing—they became raging discontent when I finally decided he hoaxed me!

I could understand muzzling exorcized demons; no righteous man wanted an alliance with Satan! But he shouldn't muzzle the very people who personally profited from his power and could advertise his worth! If he didn't want to be honored, why intentionally make himself a celebrity?

Even the few times rabbi ordered a testimony from someone he helped only deepened the inconsistency. I remember especially Jairus' urgent appeal for rabbi to hurry before his daughter died. As we proceeded to his house, a woman with a hemorrhage touched rabbi's garment—and he instantly stopped and made a scene.

How inappropriate. First, because of the throng. He could easily have kept the miracle to himself since no one but he and she *knew*. Second, with Jairus desperate for teacher's help before his daughter died, he shouldn't tarry. He nevertheless wasted precious moments till she confessed. Third, Jairus' anxiety turned to wailing when rabbi's delay caused his daughter's death—teacher even felt it necessary to quiet him with an appeal to faith. I thought, *rabbi, if you hadn't needlessly delayed, you could have prevented his grief.*

Taking his favorite trio to the house, he raised the girl, then strictly warned the parents to suppress the news. Though it could hardly happen, with mourners already at the house grieving her death! When people later saw her outside, with her playmates, they would perforce ask how.

On the way to Jairus', teacher demanded recognition of his ability, yet in the house stifled information about the same ability. He demanded publicity for the lesser miracle—unseen at that— from a woman no one knew, and obscurity for the greater miracle, important because of Jairus' community stature. Shouldn't he at least be consistent, keeping everyone, or no one silent? Did he seek a *little* fame, but abhor the *much* his works rapidly brought? Not only wouldn't they keep silent, they *couldn't*. Who could decipher this strange man— who intentionally put himself on a pedestal, then refused to be idolized!

It never ceased being an issue with me; or failed to create tension in me until I found it increasingly disturbing and eventually unacceptable. While making a colossal impression, rabbi obviously didn't consider himself a spiritual spectacle!

I became an implacable opponent when he refused to capitalize on the greatest mass miracle in Israel since manna fell in the desert. He instantaneously touched at least ten thousand people when he fed 5000 men. Every other miracle had concerned individuals or small groups, but this sparked passions on a national scale. Who but God's prophet could produce such results from his personal resources? Admiration pulsed through the crowd like blood through arteries; by conquering their hunger they wanted him as king.

Instead...I still remember my fury...he dismissed us and the crowd! He didn't even *try* to capitalize on their extremism, though it could have convinced the authorities that they had to seriously contend with him. Anyone who could muster an army of 10,000 people with one miracle had to be considered a powerful friend if accommodated, a dangerous foe if alienated.

Rabbi's refusal that day killed my interest in him, and everything he did afterwards systematically alienated instead of reconciling me. I grew *hardened* by every teaching and miracle, however stirring, spectacular or provocative. Doubt surfaced and choked faith. Despair burgeoned and destroyed hope. Where the eleven saw light I saw darkness; where they grew enthralled, I grew appalled! I couldn't adjust my perspectives; I knew he wouldn't adjust his. There I began my fatal plunge into what I considered his irreversible failures. In his denial of *Israel's* cherished hopes anchored *my* disaffection.

Then it was back to the third of four retirements from public life, for rest and private teaching, as though rabbi wanted to prepare us for something mysterious. I thought it more of the same old trick: besieging us with hope, then stealing away like barbarians before the Romans.

We went far north, through Phoenicia, then east towards Mt Hermon. Like taking a holiday, we reveled in the beauties proliferating everywhere in the mountain meadows teeming with wildlife, an emergent Jordan gurgling from the marshes, beginning its rollicking journey south.

Entering Herod Philip's jurisdiction, we avoided Antipas, who had already raised questions about Jesus being a resurrected Baptist. In the Decapolis rabbi again healed a deaf man, then ordered him hushed. Why *bother* by this time, knowing it wouldn't work? And if he feared Herod Antipas, wouldn't Philip also become suspicious? Would any place in Israel or surrounding territory be safe? Wouldn't he then have to leave Israel altogether and teach the Gentiles? And were these retirements an introduction to his leaving Israel and exiling himself to the Gentile world, using our exposure to its prevalent Greek culture to prepare us? But how could he expect us to desert our own people for those heathen? Where did that leave me, who had once considered him the likeliest possible candidate for Messiah; and where did it leave Israel, which desperately needed one?

After a short visit to Dalmanutha, we withdrew for a fourth time toward Mt. Hermon. With its massive shoulders rising above, rabbi raised the question Israel had been speculating for two years: "Who do people say I am?"

Do you really care?, I asked myself. *Have you ever shown concern for public opinion? Or are you now disenchanted with the way your ministry has turned? After all, here we are, far away from your power base in either Galilee or Judea, avoiding Antipas and the Pharisees...are you now convinced you've strayed from your mission?*

I had shared minimally as the disciples previously discussed rabbi. Hopelessly hypnotized, though understanding him no better than I, they summoned faith to explain his consistent betrayals of their hopes. Indeed, his every failure to meet their messianic expectations made them increasingly confident he was the Messiah. Like them, people throughout Israel had concluded that this powerful man was anyone from a resurrected John the Baptist to a reincarnated Elijah or Jeremiah.

When, in private sessions, Simon finally declared his belief in Jesus as the Messiah and the Son of God, I cravenly choked back my disgust and agreed with the rest. What else could I do? Why dispute with them? Why disturb their innocence? Should I have left, after all I had invested? I had learned to play the game: publicly accept it all, privately deny every word! Smile at the right time, add a nodded agreement when called—and keep my own counsel, as rabbi kept his, determined to *become* the consummate actor I felt he innately *was*!

Then too, I still harbored hope. Their belief contained the basis on which rabbi's mistakes could still be retrieved and the kingdom established. If I stayed, I might somehow influence his thinking and decisions. Naturally, I could never confront him. Who was I to beard the lion when no intellectual in Israel had? But I could offer suggestions at appropriate times. So I decided to linger until I saw no hope at all. I could always leave!

After Simon made our confession, I nearly snorted at rabbi's promise that Simon would be the rock on which Jesus built his church. *Peter*, he called him, not the usual *Simon*. Had Simon earned rabbi's encomium by his pronouncement? Had I known that, I would have made it! He *did* sweep his eyes over everyone, letting us know we all shared Simon's promise.

Still, it seemed absurd. After all his criticism of us, he would build his kingdom on our lives? And so strong it would overcome death? We who couldn't earn his minimum respect were suddenly stalwart enough to build a kingdom death couldn't resist?

Unlike the rest, I refused that idiocy. *Had he suddenly changed?*, they wondered. *Would he finally acknowledge the existence of a kingdom he for two years defiantly refused to admit? Would he now affirm concepts he had spent the past protesting? Would he now definitively determine his direction in life, then take it?*

Of course not, fools!—instead he insisted that no one be told of their confession! No one!! If he were the Son of God,

shouldn't everyone, everywhere, be told? Shouldn't the authorities be the first ones told? If he were the Son of God, the
reason his miracles had been possible, shouldn't he be na-
tionally acclaimed and followed?

He had gotten into such a habit of denial that it became a
pattern!—though this clearly exceeded all past prohibitions.
What every Israelite longed to hear he wanted cloaked in the
same silence he wrapped around his miracles. It didn't make
sense at all! Would he found a kingdom of thirteen people, one
of whom had already become a secret rebel? The eleven were
convinced; wouldn't nearly everyone else be; couldn't he even
yet redeem himself with me? And with the power to perform
miracles, could anyone stop him?

As always, he adamantly refused our appeals. The eleven
at last had a taste of what I had swallowed the past year. They
saw their joy demolished as it rose! It only reinforced my conclusion that rabbi had no intention of building anything. He
loved to talk, to dream, to fantasize, but not to take action that
mattered. The others stood aghast. I smirked, grumped
knowingly, and turned away!

Then, while I had thought myself beyond shock by this
most inexplicable man, his next words appalled even me. He
began to discuss his death! At a time like that! When he
should have said, "Since you men believe in me, my people
will now accept me," he foretold suffering and rejection.
When it seemed he would see the confession as the distin-
guishing imprimatur on his ministry, the formidable vanguard
that would become an irresistible host as we marched
southward, picking up supporters along the way until, by the
multiple thousands, rabbi could force his way into Jerusalem
for coronation, he deflated everyone by talking of his death and
of some nonsense about rising the third day.

Preposterous! Obliterating! It left us stunned as he walked
off a short distance, as if communing with his fate. No vestige
of hope remained. I *knew* he couldn't be trusted! He offered
hope to the hopeless like a mirage to the thirsty, with the same
bitter result.

The men knew one thing, however: they didn't want him to
die. Actually *none* of us wanted that! Since Simon had been
so fortunate in declaring rabbi's identity, everyone, including

myself, agreed he should carry our misgivings over to rabbi, now standing twenty yards away. "Would he please reconsider his death threats?", we wanted to know.

We should never have chosen Simon. I can see it yet...the arrogant fool...taking rabbi forcefully by the arm; *had he gone mad, acting like a master with a misguided student?*, then correcting where we expected him to *plead!*

Praise had swollen Simon's self-esteem, not his brain! *Rabbi, you chose the wrong man to publicly applaud!* Had Simon's egotism not eroded his good sense, he would have remembered that rabbi never accepted *instruction*, let alone *correction!*

Still, the way he responded terrified us! He looked past Simon to us—we dropped our heads; then turned back to him—we raised them again in time to hear every hard word, "Satan, get away from me!" The suddenly-demoralized Simon instantly withered. Speechless, all color gone, he backed unsteadily to us, head down! The strutting rooster became a peeping chick!

He called Simon the same name he called me weeks before! *Would Simon call rabbi Messiah and Son of God now?*, I petulantly wondered.

I hardly had time to savor Simon's humiliation, for teacher next so enraged me I wanted to walk over and slap him! As if he hadn't harmed Simon and us enough...and angered by our desire to keep him alive, he called together people in the area and warned of *their* death. It wasn't enough for him to die, or for the Twelve to die, **everyone** who followed him had to die! How detestable! Denying hope to Israel! Intimidating potential followers!

Our people had suffered under a succession of foreign powers, and now one of our own countrymen threatened more of the same if we followed him? Enough Jews had died! Varus had killed our people years before, deepening our hatred of his master on the Tiber. I wanted a Messiah who could at least promise life with Rome humiliated and destroyed.

Every previous Messiah had agreed that some *could* die fighting Rome, but others would live to defeat them. But Jesus demanded everyone's *death,* but said nothing about fighting Romans in the process, or why dying was necessary.

I wanted reason from rabbi and got absurdity! I wanted freedom from Rome and got slavery to self-denial! If I hadn't broken with him before, I would have then! If I hadn't already decided, that would have forced me to consult the authorities!

I congratulated myself: *You haven't confounded me, rabbi! I knew you would retreat just when a breakthrough was imminent! The eleven finally have a dose of your reality, rabbi. You can't be trusted. You don't know what you want and can't possibly cast a clear vision for us!*

On our way back through Galilee rabbi continued to discourse on his death, obsessed with it, as if he couldn't say enough about it! While it didn't bother me, it broke their hearts. Tears filled their eyes, they walked dejectedly, their faces maps of despair. The wounds he had inflicted on me had healed, leaving only scars. And I couldn't forget what those scars cost me! But the others were so dependent on him they couldn't face the prospect!

Welcome to the real world of rabbi, gentlemen, I sullenly thought!

After touring with the fifty-eight laymen rabbi sent into Judea ahead of him, we returned flush with the assurance that we *had* performed miracles never before seen in Israel— **without** seeing any "privilege" rabbi assured was ours! If we were so blessed, as he insisted, how had it accrued? We still traveled by foot, existed hand to mouth, often at largesse of women, and had no acceptance by the national leadership. By what sleight of hand did rabbi intend to translate our continuing poverty into power and his continuing contradictions into consequence?

A few weeks later I heard him claim to be greater than Solomon and Jonah, yet *saw* only a distinct servant-complex that spurned every vestige of greatness! How could he *state* such prerogatives but never *claim* them? Leadership had privileges equal to its responsibility; and while I felt rabbi had incontestably expressed leadership, and continued to accept its obligations, he resolutely scorned its entitlement.

Of course, his self-denial increased the crowds' adulation. Indeed, his fame grew with his refusal to capitalize on it. While they insisted that he accept his destiny—and he remained a man who wouldn't run if nominated as Messiah, and wouldn't serve if elected—they considered his every refusal a reason to keep insisting! He continued to *pretend* to an office he had every qualification to fill and lacked only the will to claim. I had to force a showdown.

RETROSPECT

As I sit and ponder, did I draw the wrong conclusions? Didn't rabbi anchor a precision honesty in a sea of speculative guile, where all Israelites desperately fished for hope?

Given his instinctive awareness of people's needs, who am I to say he was wrong when he demanded a witness from the woman with a hemorrhage while ordering everyone else silenced? By forcing her to confess the healing he may have revealed an important element in faith: if we insist on keeping our faith in God silent, we must necessarily make it public. For, as I can testify, silence kills faith as surely as constriction kills prey.

Maybe the teachers who counseled against speculating the Messiah's coming were right: it couldn't be predicted! After all, we had many guesses, and many failures for our efforts! Yes, we would be expected to determine from the *evidence* of his signs and teachings, but did that mean *we* would determine the signs and teachings? Did it necessarily relate to bountiful harvests, luxurious living and domination of Gentiles? Was Messiah a slave to our definition, or free to interpret himself? After, all, wouldn't speculation only make Messiah's appearance more difficult, forcing him to slash through all our pre-conceived opinions and convictions to bare his truth? As much as I wanted him to go in my direction, others wanted him to go in theirs! Give everyone the right to determine his kingdom, and rabbi would soon have no definitive say in it. Perhaps the only way he could retain control was to keep all decision-making to himself.

And...being so exalted, would he seek our counsel, or keep his own? Would he be at the mercy of contemporary views, or in possession of God's own? Did I, the hard-headed man of facts and figures, unable to be convinced against my will, unable to be conned by the magician, actually fall to Satan's oldest lie: that I determined the impact of God's word? Did I repeat that mantra so often that I convinced myself of its truth, against which all my previous experience and knowledge warned me?

Rabbinical literature and synagogue teaching both stressed Messiah's exaltation, without any demand of deity within, for how could God become a man? Still, Messiah would be so *exalted* a human that little distinction could be made between them; hadn't the prophets hinted at that majesty in their holiness, and David in his prowess? Perhaps God intended believers to instinctively *know* when Messiah came. Having lived long by faith, they could be trusted to know by sight when he rewarded faith!

As much as I hate to admit it, teacher's refusal to feed the crowd after feeding the multitude was brilliant. He fed people as *expressions* of generosity, but never as a *principle* of ministry. I detested him for it then, but see the wisdom of it now. A need-meeting ministry would exhaust itself trying to accommodate needs that increased more rapidly than solutions could be found, or people could administer them. No doubt rabbi *could* have fed modern Israel as Moses had ancient Israel. But for our people to *want* food from rabbi as the basis of discipleship, as the earlier Israelites *needed* it for daily life, put us, not rabbi, in control of our religion. My question now is, not why rabbi was so reluctant to continue feeding them, but would they have been so enthused for his kingship if he had only *taught* them the day before?

He wouldn't oblige them, and I despised him for it. Now I know the impossibility of letting mortals dictate policy to religious leaders, particularly one like rabbi. If we had let him broaden us to enclose his breadth instead of trying to shrink him to our perceptions, Israel wouldn't have lost a great religious leader, and I wouldn't be here in this lonely place, distressed, depressed, ready to take my life!

Suddenly, my refusal to see rabbi as my kind of Messiah seems prodigiously stupid!

ACCEPTANCE OF UNDESIRABLES

Rabbi struck a lively rapport with every class in Israel. Never did a leader enjoy a wider range of followers from whom to choose associates. Aristocrats as avidly sought him as plebeians, foreigners as readily as Jews, Zealots as actively as Herodians.

How could an obviously peasant man feel socially comfortable with the elegant manners and refined tastes of the nation's elite? He proved it didn't take pomp to create majesty or a throne to make a king. Was it an innate royalty? Was it an inbred command presence that ruled, without wearing a commander's laurels? Was it an astute erudition his surface homespun couldn't mask, from sources we never identified, that mastered any subject he or they surfaced?

Equally puzzling, when rabbi could easily have spent the majority of his time with leaders, exchanging mutually beneficial counsel, why did he choose those who brought only problems: the mob, the Galileans, the disenfranchised? And was it worth reaching commoners if, in the process, he alienated the leaders, whom he needed to establish a lasting presence in Israel? Teacher never said, but left no doubt that he considered everyone equal, even when the common people exempted the rich and famous from rules they personally had to obey! His personal choice, let me add, not aristocratic indifference to him, made the determination. Where the leaders considered teacher their equal, he chose undesirables as his.

I should have interrogated myself: *did I want to follow a teacher who made disciples of those I wouldn't make slaves?* It became another unresolved issue dividing us.

GALILEAN DISCIPLES

First on my list of undesirables! Why overload the Twelve with those qualified to feed, not lead the nation? He should at

least have included in his religious cabinet acknowledged, sophisticated leaders from every province, with a majority from
Judea—not pack it with anonymous Galileans, all of whom
would have remained obscure without him and whose limitations made his task harder. Could that choice be traced to his
origins? Whatever his cultivation of Judeans, his social ease
among them and their esteem of him, did he feel *at home* only
among those who shared his youth, values and life perspectives?

PUBLICANS AND SINNERS

True, all messianic hopefuls recruited followers wherever
available, but who initiated the effort with the very servants of
the detested Empire radicals wanted overthrown? He even
chose one as a disciple! As the banquet at Levi's house proved,
rabbi loved their corrupt company. Perhaps he didn't know he
could keep his character while losing his reputation! And how
outrageous to call Zacchaeus a son of Abraham!   His Jewish
blood curdled when sold to Rome!
Then to scandalously use a *publican* as the example of a
person God justifies! The most visible example of corruption
in society, the hated symbol of Rome's presence in our daily
lives, who taxed everything that moved, and pushed
everything stationary so it would and they could! Why use a
man we all hated to shame one we had all been taught to
respect? Why not instead use a good Pharisee to expose the
bad Pharisee?
Rabbi consistently undervalued those responsible for
Israel's national life to prize those who merely profited by it.
As if he intended to reshape Israel into a kingdom of the blind,
deaf, dumb, crippled and leper-stricken, with himself as their
chief; to use religiously illiterate laymen, who couldn't even
get past the Court of Israel; to create a new priesthood from
those misfits!
No wonder Jesus of Nazareth would never succeed; he
didn't recognize *quality!*

SAMARITANS

I never understood how rabbi talked freely with a Samaritan slut, intentionally breaking our taboos. Then, having insufficiently offended us, he welcomed her towns-people...those corrupted heathen staunchly prejudiced for Gerizim over Moriah. He treated them like religious equals, not rebels!

He never lost his fascination with the Samaritans! When a teacher later asked to obtain eternal life, rabbi replied with a question, which the man correctly answered. However, when the man posed his own question—as always, rabbi didn't like to be interrogated—he responded with one of his stories, this time about a traveler, robbers and Jews disregarding and a hated Samaritan aiding a wounded Jew. Why brazenly deride Jews and praise Samaritans when he knew how it displeased us?

TEMPLE SOLDIERS

After the encomiums heaped on rabbi last winter, the Sanhedrin audaciously sent hardened enforcers to arrest him in the temple—in the open, crowds present, finally affirming their authority. We saw them arrive and stand at the rear of the audience, hands on short swords, ready to pounce if teacher tried to escape. Seemingly oblivious of them, he taught. And lo, he turned the Sanhedrin's shield into flint against which his words struck sparks, then flames of faith. Someone suddenly barked a command, and they left! They who came intending to arrest him wordlessly vanished into the crowds!

I have no idea how they explained their insubordination, though I'm sure the leaders sputtered their exasperation! The perfect chance to seize him— their own men sent to do it— and their enemy's teaching *converted* them! How could they ever overcome a man who *talked* their own soldiers out of arresting him?

I personally thought Jesus had impressed the wrong people! Maybe the guards heard nightingales and smelled roses when he spoke, but their overlords heard ravens and smelled Hinnom! Rabbi lacked David's genius for wooing all Israel by

first singing sweet psalms to the composers of our culture!
Until he acquired David's skill, the leadership would remain
lethal, for they could always find soldiers immune to rabbi's
charm.

The incident materialized an idea that had been floating dis-
embodied in my mind: if not one of *their* own men, could one
of *rabbi's* own men deliver him to the leaders?   While well
liked, even by his enemies, wouldn't the Sanhedrin be delighted to find rabbi enough disliked by a friend to arrange his
arrest? They had grown equally tired of his machinations and
delusions; had lost all hope in his promises; wouldn't be affected by his charm or good will or teachings! A private,
face-to-face encounter would surely disarm both sides—and
wasn't I, as the only Judean disciple, the likeliest candidate as
conciliator?

The sensation emerged like clay under a seal, emphatically
posted its presence, then as quickly receded. Yet the impression remained, waiting to be matured by events. I had
mentally committed myself to future action!

CHILDREN

Rabbi consistently preferred children to us. It first occurred
in Capernaum, after the Galilean ministry. When the question
of greatness in the kingdom arose, instigated by the arrogance
of rabbi's inner circle, he humiliated every adult present by
making a child his kingdom's model citizen.

Okay, I thought, *rabbi employed that radical illustration to
silence what has become very unpleasant competition among
the Twelve.* No more than five months later, however, he again
reproved our attempt to protect him from children. We knew
how kids romped, interrupted, demanded and distracted. We
only wanted to spare him. I should have known: he repri-
manded us and beckoned them—and while we shook our heads
in resignation they rushed at him, squealing and shrieking, surrounded him, leaned against his legs, peered into those big
brown eyes—sunlight glowing in theirs!

Then, as though we hadn't learned our lesson five months
before, he reiterated it: none of *us* qualified, but these helpless
urchins, without rights at home, were *ideal* citizens of the

kingdom. Did the man's impudence have no limits? Did he think he could continue to shock people, yet retain their interest?

ROMANS

I suppose *good* Romans exist and, leave it up to rabbi, he found one. But did it have to be a centurion, a class known for alley-cat morals and unconscionable brutality? This one did have the recommendation of Jewish elders from his town; seems he even built them a synagogue. But, then, if Romans hadn't unfairly taxed us, we could build our own synagogues! They stole our wealth, gave us a pittance in turn, and expected our praise of *their* generosity!

I suppose the man did express considerable faith in rabbi. Where the leaders wondered where rabbi got his authority, he seemed to know. Teacher said he hadn't found such faith in Israel—though he had been preaching well over a year! No one in Israel had such faith? A gentile superior to us? A Roman Gentile at that? A Roman Gentile *soldier* worst of all?

Was rabbi merely *cultivating* the man or *demeaning* Israelites, making a good impression on him at our expense? Why would I *want* to follow a Jewish teacher who implied that we were field stones and the Gentiles gold-plated jewels! Did he intend to raise his army from the very people who now subjugated Israel? Did he prefer them to his own Jewish men of renown?

It made me retch to think about it. I felt rabbi had already picked sides, and we weren't chosen. Where did that leave the people to whom God gave the Law?

GREEKS

They came to rabbi this past Monday. Now...I never saw a more unhurried, imperturbable person than rabbi. But their arrival stirred in him some powerful turmoil I couldn't identify. It was similar to, without the extremity of his weeping over Jerusalem on Sunday, but completely unlike him. It unnerved me at the time—and I wondered if he hadn't damaged the image of untouchable courage he had so carefully crafted.

And...since he came to lead Israel, why should he be shaken by
the arrival of *Greeks*?

WOMEN

When starting the second Galilean tour, teacher acquired
women supporters, humbly accepting help most rabbis would
reject, and even resent being *offered*. Why did ours have to be
so different? I hated to rely on them for financial support. It
sank beneath my dignity to have women as equals in his en-
tourage—what would people think—but to rely on them for
daily needs? Had he no common sense, ignoring the wealth
available from generous aristocrats who appreciated his intentions, knew the demands on our ministry and offered to
help?

I hated also that women found him so available to their
pleas. The feast at Simon the Pharisee's went well until the
harlot entered and somehow bypassed the guards—an inex-
cusable breach of security, since rabbi always attracted her
type! She sternly wound her way through the couches till she
came to him. Breaking emotionally, she wet his feet with her
tears, and, against all custom, removed her hair brackets and
wiped his feet in her long tresses.

Like a scroll Simon's face registered indignation toward
the woman and disgust at rabbi— feelings I shared. Yet
teacher censured Simon and commended the woman.

We no sooner left what rabbi called a nest of tradition-
bound hypocrites for a heathen land where God wasn't
worshiped at all, when a woman of the country assaulted us for
favors. How did he attract all those people?

She had a demon-infested daughter, she said—there seemed
no end of such— and wanted her cleansed. She badgered him
while we walked the streets, then brazenly entered the house
where we all reclined, bent at his couch and continued begging.
He ignored her—finally doing something right with all the
claimants on his time! After hearing as much as we could
stand, in chorus we demanded he dispatch her and her tears.
Instead he spoke to us, but clearly aiming at her, about not
being sent to anyone but the people of Israel.

Watching him and listening intently, and apparently hearing an encouragement to further dialogue, she reiterated her request: Lord, please help me!

A slight smile crossed his face...she gazed at him...he softly said, "It isn't right to feed dogs the children's food."

Had he not said it so playfully, I would have congratulated teacher for once abusing a heathen who disrespected Judaism.

My naivete knew no limits!

Her tears dried, she took courage, rose from her knees and, eyes glistening, with a touch of humor in her appeal as softly replied, "That's true Lord, but don't the dogs get scraps from the children's table?"

Rabbi broke into a grin, clapped his hands and lauded her like she was the Queen of Sheba with spice-laden camels — then granted her request!

She continued to look longingly into his eyes until he imperceptibly winked at her, then turned and clattered away, praising the God of Israel!

I sat stunned. He let himself be overwhelmed by a woman's insightful rejoinder, while all studied, scholarly arguments meant nothing to him.

How could rabbi expect his own people to love and honor him when he lavished only praise on foreigners and only denunciation on us? Would that inspire his own people to rise in his presence? No self-respecting Jewish male would have let the woman remain in the house, or even in the crowd begging his help, let alone be lavished with his immodest panegyric!

A Messiah who wasted his time *outside* Israel on *Gentile women—that* hardly met my requirements!

BLIND MEN

While in Jerusalem for Tabernacles rabbi healed a blind man, despite it being a Sabbath— or perhaps because it was. Later, hearing that the man had been excommunicated, teacher found him and urged his faithfulness. Why take time to reinforce that man but make no effort to reach the leaders? I had no explanation for this independent man! It offered another example of how he deliberately chose the weak to show only he was strong, the foolish to prove only he was wise.

Then...against all propriety, he revealed himself as Messiah to that same commoner! To him, who didn't know the difference; not to the leaders, who did! Jesus upset every scale by which I weighed my values!

I had become so jaded I didn't care—it was just one more example of rabbi's determination to recruit the people I refused to consider worthy of a second thought; a view I knew the leaders shared! Little wonder they grew increasingly settled in their determination to kill him; or that I grew equally determined to help. Rabbi simply didn't understand the times!

RETROSPECT

Wherever he went rabbi boldly critiqued his aristocratic hosts and shamelessly courted peasants. In any home, at any feast reclined any number of people capable of boosting his prospects—which he consistently declined. But not a single peasant found him unwilling or unable!

As I've pondered, I think I know why he magnified the poor over the wealthy, the powerless over the powerful, the unwashed over the bathed, those without ceremony to those schooled in it: while the helpless sought him only for help, the leaders often invited him to critique him or to make connections for the kingdom they hoped he would found.

Maybe that explains why rabbi talked about revealing God to those he pleased. He felt that the lowly and burdened, with a sense of guilt I never knew, made the best students of his teaching! People with personal woes, not ambition; those wanting release from personal problems, not from Rome; those willing to *serve*, not acquire fame, or position or political station. Maybe...!

I'm confident that he freely gave himself to the needy because they begged instead of demanded help! Knowing they couldn't deserve mercy, by pleading they received it. *That* a proud Pharisee wouldn't do! Then too, all that the poor could offer was fanatical praise for his miracles. Knowing rabbi as I do, it's really the only way they *could* repay him. Refusing all financial reimbursement, he accepted gratitude as payment in full!

What a high price to be rabbi's disciple, I had often stormed. *He offends every social rule I know, and all my personal values!* But I understand now; it was my problem, not his. Only by being among the wealthy could I sustain my ego. Teacher felt so secure that he could be among the high without feeling exalted and among the lowly without feeling debased! Oh, that I could have been like him!

I also remember how rabbi carelessly let people interfere with sleep, meals and relaxation. How irritating that even times of withdrawal became occasions for more service among the constantly-demanding crowds! After we returned from the Galilean tour, he saw our exhaustion and suggested a retirement to the eastern lake shore. The crowds anticipated our destination and began arriving as we disembarked. Rabbi couldn't say no; he began teaching, despite our fatigue.

How angry I became! It didn't surprise me that the crowds cared nothing about our health, but he should have. They never ceased clamoring for help, even when he had to stay busy late at night or rise early in the morning, but what about us? We had a limit to our energy, if rabbi didn't. And he had a commitment to the cause I personally lacked!

Is this what discipleship is going to be, I often wondered, *meeting never-ending needs, responding to never-ending requests? This isn't why I follow rabbi: constant pressure, maddening interruptions. It seems to energize him, but it depletes me. This doesn't portend the conquering political power I imagined would be mine—servants carrying my litter, obeying my every command. With rabbi, I'm the servant and these commoners the masters!*

Now, as I *reconsider*, whenever the crowds brought heavier burdens, greater vitality invariably came to us. It never occurred to me to ask how, when, or why, but...could it have been God's response? As nerve-wracking as it often seemed then, I now realize how our exhaustion turned to exhilaration as we helped him care for the crowds. Why did I focus on the problems of those days and not appreciate the pleasures?

Most in the aristocracy mistakenly felt they already owned the ecstasy glittering in the eyes of undesirables rabbi helped. His very accessibility gave those unfortunates hope; his triumph over every problem they brought *matured* it! It comes

to me now...too late. I suddenly understand his willingness to
help the forlorn: why waste himself on men who felt no need of
the mercy he brought when he could replenish himself giving it
to those longing to receive? I now ask myself, "Fool, doesn't
that make sense? Wouldn't you love to feel his embrace around
you now?"

FAILURE TO VALUE FRIENDS AND FAMILY

Given his self-possessed mien and persona, it may have been normal for rabbi to depreciate those who loved him. Or for his utter disregard of forms, ceremonies, small talk and sentiment to make him appear less concerned than he really was.

Nevertheless, he wasted no time distancing himself from others. On his way to Galilee from Judea after the first temple cleansing, he remarked on how little he could trust peoples' opinions: and they, the "common people" to whom he would devote his life, wild about him!

A much later incident proved that he hadn't changed. Overwhelmed by his teaching, a woman rhapsodized, "Blessed is the mother who gave you birth and nursed you." She praised him the best she could but, refusing to be complimented, he turned it into an insult. It certainly abolished his mother's relevance to him. Important only for bringing him into the world, he wouldn't consult her for advice or share adoration with her!

These proved just the vanguard of seven groups rabbi's unsettling remoteness and unconcern offended.

JUDEANS

At the last Feast of Tabernacles he disillusioned the Judeans he could have definitively recruited as followers—the very people he ordinarily couldn't convince. As was his custom, he first enraged the Pharisees by lecturing them about his exalted place with God. Then, turning to the people, whom he never failed to fascinate, he began the deepest discussion I had ever heard: about his going away and them staying; about his being from another and they from this world; and, amazing effrontery, that unless they believed in him, they would die in sin!

When they asked clarification of the I AM person he claimed to be—they had a right to know since it implied **so**

much—he evasively and ambiguously replied with references to someone truthful who had sent him, to whom he had been faithful.

He then said he would be recognized as the I AM when he had been "lifted up," whatever that meant. Accustomed as *I* had become to his enigmas, I had no idea, but it enchanted certain Jews, including Pharisees, and they admitted faith in him! Knowing his methods, I urged reserve. They would learn that rabbi would make them twice as angry as he ever made them glad.

According to my prediction, he first disillusioned, then alienated them. He spoke of: setting sinners free; their threats against his life; their inability to believe; his conquest of death...and finally, his superiority to Abraham, even claiming, "your father Abraham rejoiced at the thought of seeing my day; he saw it and was glad."

They could hardly find words for sputtering their rejoinder. "You are not fifty years old...and you have seen Abraham?"

Everyone stood stupefied as he calmly and unpretentiously declared, "I tell you the truth..., before Abraham was born, **I AM!**"

As if awakening from a stupor, they understood at last; the I AM he referred to was HIMSELF! Not only did he have God as his Father; he was actually GOD! The words every Jew revered so much he would hardly say them...and the Galilean superciliously claimed them for himself!

I recoiled when they picked up stones kept in the temple for the very purpose of executing blasphemers, to stone the blasphemer! And these the very people who had just professed faith in him! If even they wanted to kill him, how much more the leaders who had so much more to lose by his arrogance?

For one of the few times in his ministry, rabbi *intentionally* disappeared into the masses. As we followed, forming a shield around him, I noticed his utter fearlessness—as if they wouldn't dare attack him! He had more confidence than I. I feared the people themselves would kill him, before the leaders could.

Rabbi left that day as if he had done his day's work by making everyone possible as angry as possible. As if, having alienated the one city he should have *cultivated,* he disregarded the damage to himself and the God he claimed to serve. *Maybe that was his plan*, I dejectedly thought: *to eliminate all his friends by ones and twos and dozens and hundreds until he had no friends at all in the city except the Twelve—and I no longer his friend; instead, willing to make the hardest decision I had ever faced: to save teacher from the consequences his mistakes portended.*

BIOLOGICAL FAMILY

Rabbi consistently mistreated his nuclear family, the inevitable result of his teaching that all families and livelihoods be abandoned to discipleship.

In the middle of his Galilean campaign, while bitterly debating the leadership over the source of his authority, his family came to quietly take custody of him. He had continually ignored their warnings of disaster if he and the Pharisees continued to butt heads like mountain sheep in rut. For his own safety the family had to rescue him!

They found the house packed and people standing at the open windows and in the courtyard, the overflow lounging in the street. What were they to do? They couldn't contact him personally, yet felt embarrassed for him—possessed as he seemed with a messianic complex. And they felt badly treating a grown man like an erring child who didn't understand the tumult he caused. Nevertheless, responsibility to family honor forced them to send their intention mouth by mouth, ring by ring of people. Soon, back from him came his reply mouth by mouth, ring by ring of people, making sure everyone heard. Without so much as *recognizing* them, let alone their authority over him, he treated them as strangers. "He says to tell you that his mother and brothers are those who hear and keep God's word." As if they didn't!

Was that any way to talk to your mother? Who was she if not a faithful disciple of Moses? And didn't his siblings all attend synagogue services? Couldn't he have at least sent a disciple out with such blockbuster news? Did he have to splatter their pride all over Galilee?

The brothers later proved how alienated they had become. In two years of ministry he continued to roam Galilee instead of taking his showy miracles and teachings to Judea. Make it in Jerusalem, and he made it anywhere in Israel, they insisted. Ignore Jerusalem, and all his efforts would be futile, produce frustration and might ultimately cost his life. Jerusalem was the heart of the messianic kingdom, as all the failed Galilean revolutionaries had discovered. As a Judean, I knew they were right.

Their objections only hardened him to his mission and to his certainty of their ignorance. Let rabbi go his own way, I decided. I would follow him to the end, which I didn't think could be that distant. But it was becoming increasingly clear to me that he would hate what he found there. If he wouldn't take counsel from his own family, those who had *nothing but* his welfare at heart, who could influence him? Who could save this unusual man from the mistakes that kept turning everyone who confronted him into an active enemy or, at best, into a non-vocal friend? After you have alienated enough people, who's left to help you? Who's left but sworn enemies who aim to harm and would retaliate for all the times he had publicly shamed and humiliated them?

I would stay, not because I saw promise, and not because rabbi forecast a change in his intransigent singularity, but because I wanted to be able to say, "I told you so," and to help rebuild the dreams his strong-headed misdirection had destroyed.

RESIDENTS OF NAZARETH

Initial admiration expressed by the people on his first visit quickly turned to dismay, suspicion, distrust and hatred when he declared the superiority of Gentiles over Jews.

We accompanied him on his second visit at the end of the great Galilean campaign. Though no longer truculent towards him, they expressed only astonishment at, not faith in, the success he achieved. Seeing him as a reflection of themselves, they resented his climb to heights they had never reached and questioned *how* he had climbed there. Offering no explanation, he performed a few miracles as evidence against their obduracy.

Nothing worked. They didn't give him a chance.

Their response nearly shamed me for the charges I had mentally made against him for the past months. I almost shouted defiance at them, *think what this man is doing for you, performing miracles to underscore his claims; think of the people who wanted a miracle and didn't receive it; who walked for miles to see rabbi just so he could help them—and he's gone out of his way to offer you a special dispensation; take advantage of it while you can!*

A second perspective cooled my wrath against them, however. Couldn't he have shown patience with their demands and understanding of their reluctance precisely because of his background? Instead of taking extremes measures to pacify his home town—just because it *was* his home town, allowing for the problems *that* created—he used their skepticism as an excuse to perform those few miserable miracles. Maybe he would have convinced them had he fed the entire village as he had the multitudes. He went out of his way to reach undesirables all over Galilee, Judea, Samaria and into Gentile territory, but wouldn't make an exception for the native village that provided a quarter century of companionship and values!

PLAYING FAVORITES AMONG THE TWELVE

He chose only six disciples in the beginning, not incorporating the other half-dozen in the nucleus for as much as ten months into his Galilean ministry, though we were equally faithful. Then he made three of the band his inner circle.

I adamantly opposed favoritism! Weren't we all in this together? Didn't we share common hopes and faith? *And*, if anyone should have been included in such a group, shouldn't it have been the *Treasurer*, with all his responsibilities?

And did they ever remind us of the honor, irking everyone, *even* placid Andrew, who seldom got offended with anyone about anything, let alone with his brother, whom he clearly adored! If he were going to play favorites, shouldn't he at least choose men who would wear the honor gracefully?

The flagrant result of rabbi's favoritism backfired after the trio saw the incredible brightness surrounding him that night on Mt. Hermon. The experience obviously meant more to them than rabbi realized; they couldn't wait to recount and reiterate the experience: how it overwhelmed them; what it meant for their future; how important they had become.

We heatedly disputed their interpretation, continuing the argument on our return to Capernaum—more contentiously than we intended because, once there, teacher questioned us about it. After a long silence, which the trio could have broken by apologizing, I finally gathered the courage to ask—after telling what the three had said to us—"Rabbi, who *is* greatest in the kingdom?"

Without so much as a *reference* to the troublemakers—I couldn't help but think that if I had made the boast, teacher would have devastated me—he took a child in his arms and used him as a model citizen of his kingdom.

Last winter rabbi finally learned the dangers of coddling his cousins. Despite rabbi's earlier rebuke, they continued to dream, based on their mountain experience. Combined with their biological relationship with rabbi, as cousins on their mothers' side—Salome a sister to Mary—they demanded dominance even Simon hadn't requested!

Never had favoritism looked so ugly, though any of the nine could see it coming, the brothers wore their privileges so poorly. Like skillful politicians, they used their mother—they knew how kindly rabbi treated women—to introduce their request, then they made the actual appeal: let us be your primary ministers when you ascend the throne!

Livid when we heard it, we considered it shameless exploitation of their blood relationship! Hadn't he repeatedly promised equality for everyone, with children the ideal subjects? Had the rules changed, with family connections now the litmus test of rabbi's kingdom?

And how could they have heard rabbi talk of *dying*, then demand *prominence* in his kingdom? Could they so easily dismiss teachings they didn't understand, especially when contradicting their passion for glory?

What infuriated everyone, however, was rabbi's reply. If anyone else, even Peter, had made the request, instead of his aunt or cousins, rabbi would have blown a sirocco in his face. I'd hate to think what he would have done to me!

I stood apart with some indifference, *knowing* he would respond passively to their outrage, even if he rejected their appeals. Wouldn't want to offend his darlings; after all their mommies were sisters! Their ego couldn't be satisfied, but don't upset them!

Indeed, I had become convinced that power in this kingdom would be centered in a few, whatever rabbi said to the contrary—and as one of the many, I would never be one of the few!

MY OWN MINORITY STATUS

I'm a minority, perceived as a minority, made to feel a minority. They will swear it was only my perception, and rabbi would vehemently deny it, but as a token Judean in what was obviously a Galilean endeavor, I never won their approval. They had time for each other and talked to each other *past me*, as if I weren't between them. And teacher spent most of his time in Galilee, with his own kind, ignoring the needs of Judea, especially Jerusalem.

Yes, they asked me to be treasurer—even taking their request to rabbi, who quickly approved. But, after all, my business background made me the obvious choice; and anyway, their bequest, with all its pretended sincerity, offered slight compensation for more serious neglect. And no concession to their guilty consciences could reconcile my estrangement.

All I ever wanted, and never received because of their prejudices, was to be equally important to Jesus, to prove myself as good a man as he had. I never got it. I always felt like the tail that would never wag the dog!

I finally swore to show them all, avenging myself for their prejudice and disrespect!

ACCUSATIONS AGAINST THE TWELVE

In a way, I thought it well for rabbi to criticize us, or he would have had no occasion to mention us. Whatever the circumstance, he never failed to censure our shortcomings. And, while we had plenty, he didn't *encourage* learning by stressing our *deficiency*. Positive reinforcement would at least have made us willing to learn.

Or was I was the only one who felt degraded by his dumbing-down tactics?

After one of the fullest days I ever experienced, we sailed to the lake's eastern shore. We all fell exhausted in the boat, rabbi especially worn from his teaching. While he slept undisturbed we awakened when the storm hit and tried every strategy to save ourselves. Only when doom threatened did we awaken him. Groggy with exhaustion he sat up, looked around sleepily, then spoke *quietly* to the wind and waves like a scholar to his students. Astonishingly, the wind instantly ceased and the water instantly calmed!

Who was this man who could *so persuasively control the elements?*

Once fully awake, he chided us for being fearful that we'd drown in the worst storm the fishermen had ever seen. *Was he cranky because we disturbed his sleep?*

Then there was his teaching. We had heard sermons in the synagogues that were so appallingly dry they could be used to mop up water, but at least they could be understood. As exciting as teacher was, he often left everyone mystified, especially when he used parables. When we asked for simple explanations, he criticized our inadequacy, which we confessed, but which I at least considered his responsibility to remove. I repeatedly interrogated myself: *though he considers us dunces for not comprehending him, is the real problem us or him? Why blame our incapacity when the problem might well be his obscurity!*

Rabbi's reprimand of our embarrassing failure to exorcize the demon below the mountain incensed me, and still does! While the father firmly held the lad, Levi tried and failed to heal him. We all took turns standing over him. As each tried, and failed, the Pharisees sarcastically strafed our desperation: "Feel like prophets of Baal, do you? Yell louder! Cut yourselves with knives, you hirelings of that false prophet!"

Rabbi returned and solved the problem. When we later asked why we failed, he berated our lack of faith instead of condemning the Pharisees for callously badgering us in his absence. Couldn't he have taken pity on our effort instead of taking aim at our failure? We didn't *want* to fail, giving the Pharisees the opportunity to make us look like fools!

When he admitted that such challenges were reserved for his power alone, a disturbing question posed itself to me: *then why was our lack of faith to blame? If we're unable to succeed, why castigate us when we don't? And why can't you occasionally invoke extenuating circumstances on our behalf? That courtesy would hearten as your reproofs enervate us!*

Or did I alone take such exception with rabbi's tiring references to our blunders?

Another rebuke occurred when James and John told about the man we had seen casting out demons in rabbi's name. As a stranger to us, we all agreed when the brothers silenced him. Teacher would surely want to keep his power confined to the Twelve.

Even there rabbi fooled us, saying that no one speaking in his name could at the same time speak evil of him. Amazing contradiction! He demanded that *we*, the Twelve, not tell he was Messiah, but didn't care if a complete stranger preached and healed in his name? If he feared *we* would misinterpret his messianic personality, how could he expect perfect strangers to adequately represent him?

On the last journey to Jerusalem rabbi's discussion with the young ruler finally determined my future action, removing any remaining doubts about the existence of the kingdom and my role in it. Rabbi insisted that it was easier for a camel to go through a needle's eye than for a rich man to enter Heaven. The novel idea startled everyone. If the wealthy couldn't enter Heaven, who could? Then Simon, for once asking a penetrating question, spoke for us all: "We have left everything to follow you." In that statement, his and our unspoken question: *if not the rich, what about the intentional poor? Do they have any right to expect rewards in Heaven? And what about the Twelve, since we all gave up so much to follow?*

Teacher replied with a parable about laborers in the vineyard who were all considered equal by the owner. No one received special benefits. Not those with him from the beginning! Not those who had borne the heat of the day laboring for him! Not those who surrendered their own careers while they followed a *promise*!

I would never be reduced to equality with anyone, not even among the eleven disciples! Not I, who had borne the anxiety

of paying the bills when the treasury shrank as expenditures
ballooned. I demanded rewards equal to my sacrifices! And if
rabbi wouldn't *guarantee* that return, I would seek it some
other way, even if it cost him more than he could afford to pay!
He punctured all remaining hope with that teaching, *hardening*
my already complete alienation.

JOHN THE BAPTIST

The man who preceded rabbi. Introduced him to Israel.
Acclaimed the unknown Galilean.   Made his acceptance sure.
Refused to take umbrage when outclassed by his preaching.
Provided his original disciples.

Yet, when enforced idleness surfaced doubts in John's
mind, and he sent messengers to inquire about his plans, rabbi
expressed no sympathy for John's imprisonment, no appreciation of his ministry and no exception for the savage harm
incarceration inflicted on him.

Yes, he offered convincing proof of his identity as he understood it. Yes, he indirectly summoned John to perseverance
in his original faith in order to verify his original evaluation.
But didn't John deserve more than that a curt injunction that I
thought amounted to censure?   Human beings have limits; I
certainly learned that in my experience with teacher!   Didn't
John, of all people, deserve to *know*, just so he wouldn't have
to *guess* at rabbi's intentions?

What if their places had been reversed? Would Jesus have
wanted to be left all alone by the man he admired most of all,
whose kind word meant more than volumes from others? Was
that the way he would react to all who expressed doubts about
and asked questions of him?

THEN, and I never forgave rabbi for this: after the men
left, he offered compliments to John! After it was too late—
and am I an expert in having Jesus offer me too little, too
late!—with the messengers out of earshot, teacher conceded
John's greatness—perhaps to neutralize the undertones of
disgust in the crowd about his initial response.

RETROSPECT

Perhaps rabbi heard the man behind John the Baptist's question, where I heard only the question. Until rabbi appeared I had never seen a tougher man than John. His very presence reeked of the desert and isolation, of rugged strength and ultimatums. Rabbi's surface serenity masked the same rugged manhood! Everyone soon realized that both had molten cores their faces reflected! And, as kindred spirits, they understood each other as only kindred spirits could. Maybe he refused to forthrightly answer John's question because he knew John's resolution. John would believe, even if God didn't answer his request. And if Jesus had that much faith in John, who am I to dispute him?

As for what I considered his mistreatment of Mary and her children when they came to take rabbi away: shouldn't they of all people have *known*, having him from birth, what the Twelve *learned*? And if he treated his mother like any other woman that day, he treated every woman as a mother, sister or daughter. He simply had no time for or interest in earthly relationships. That he considered the Twelve his spiritual family, we all knew. We understood, however: while we alone lived with him, no one knew better than we how far above and beyond us he was. And if from us, his chosen disciples, how **not** beyond everyone else in Israel?

Last fall I condemned rabbi for unnecessarily alienating the Judeans. Had he been merely more circumspect in his claims, I thought, he might have cultivated rather than nullifying their interest. Now I wonder: hadn't even the peasants of Judea expressed a remarkable disdain for him? Hadn't I? Judeans not only considered Galileans undignified but unduly influenced by the Hellenism of their province. Knowing that inbred reserve, rabbi may have decided to spend little time and effort there, whatever his brothers thought. After all, how was their religious experience broader than his? And if Jerusalem constituted their "world," hadn't rabbi's teachings by then proved him a man of his own world?

Little wonder the Nazarenes soared into rage on his first and into awe-struck wonder on his second visit! For thirty years he had proved to be only someone *different* from them, with an indefinable mystery they couldn't decipher. Then suddenly he became the revolutionary figure effortlessly healing and exorcising, caustically challenging the leaders and audaciously confronting listeners with astonishingly original, mature teaching.

The Nazarenes couldn't understand: why hadn't he been that open with them as a boy, recruiting their interest and discipleship? Why remain silent all those years, raising suspicions of his motives, rousing criticisms of his often dreamy-eyed distant look? And why hadn't he begun his rise in Nazareth, which could have used the fame he naturally brought everything associated with him?

But I can't critique them, for I became like them, questioning, doubting and finally rejecting because I couldn't understand him either! If Joseph didn't, Mary didn't, his brothers and sisters didn't, his own townspeople didn't and the eleven didn't, how could I—and how dare I demand it as the price of continued discipleship! Did I think *I* had become the Messiah?

I still can't understand rabbi's resort to the trio on critical occasions. What need did they fill in his life or ministry? Whatever it *was*, it *wasn't* to seek their counsel, gain their insights or share his ideas with them. They were equally mystified. He never divulged himself to them, they said, when we discussed it in private. Even with them, they repeatedly said, he retained his distance—warm while aloof, open while inscrutable.

And, as even I would now have to admit, while all of us had equal access to him, everyone immensely comfortable in his presence, I alone withstood him, demanding answers from, not intimacy with him. And all but myself continued to feel relevant to him, despite his clear independence of us. They were constantly amazed how he could be so superior to them, yet make them feel so essential. Everyone but myself, I'm now ashamed to say! I removed myself from him gradually until by last Spring I had rejected him. By my choice, not at his insistence! He excluded me from the three and, in anger, I excluded myself from the Twelve!

When will mortals ever comprehend him? And could his mystery be true precisely because he expressed it? From anyone else nonsense, even blasphemy, but in him eminently believable! If his whole persona seemed so preposterous as to be impossible, who other than rabbi gave it substance? I can't say he was what he claimed; I certainly can't say he wasn't. I can say he was different from any other teacher I ever heard; different from the prophets I've read; different from the Moses we had from birth been taught to venerate.

WHO WAS JESUS OF NAZARETH? Perhaps succeeding generations will be able to determine what ours can only estimate. I'm now haunted by the possibility that I may have destroyed Israel's best hope for the Messiah! With him before Pilate, on the way to death, who will now come and lead us? If someone does, how could he be superior to rabbi? If he were, would he have any better success with our people? Have we not systematically rejected those regularly sent from God to our generations?

And would he find in *his* disciple band another like *me* who would become so disenchanted he would betray him to authorities who couldn't tolerate his originality? Yes, we have a history of rejecting our prophets. But did any prophet have the misfortune of being betrayed by one of his own followers?

It's amazing how much clearer I see what I've done now that rabbi stands condemned! Did it take this to awaken me— when it's too late, for me as well as for him? How mournfully sad this confession, and how I wish I weren't making it, so one could know the fool I feel myself for having made my decision. My choice, then, but how I despise it now! My choice—and oh, how I would change it if only I could!

SPIRITUAL EMPHASIS

John the Baptist clearly saw himself as Messiah's herald. Like servants before their kings, John announced Messiah's imminent appearance. As a prophet he awakened Israel to forgiveness so Messiah's coming would be constructive, not judgmental. If we didn't accept the baptism of water that saved, John warned, we would suffer Messiah's baptism of fire that consumed! With the rest I heard John's spiritual emphasis. Like many who heard, while he kept saying one thing, I kept hearing another, different thing.

A cadre of John's disciples transferred to Jesus when John announced him as the "lamb of God who takes away the sin of the world." As a disciple of John, then an early follower of Jesus of Nazareth, I made enough of an impression on him that he accepted me as a member of the larger group of followers, then called me into the Twelve some months later. I at first saw rabbi as a political gold mine but eighteen months later declared him an empty shaft. Whatever heat he preached cast no warmth on my opinions. The prosperity, wealth and power accruing to me as Jesus rose and Rome fell, would never be mine. During these fateful months I stored unresolved doubts, frustrations and angers, concluding that Jesus had promised the world without delivering an inch of territory.

After feeding the 5000 men, the awful truth of his spiritual emphasis inched its way across my mind until it fully eclipsed faith in him. Yet, rabbi's constant, obvious spiritual emphasis, by miracles or teaching, demonstrated by his cleansing of the temple, then verified in his interview with Nicodemus, had warned me from the first: I would be disappointed if I looked to him as the Messiah patriots expected or the bureaucracy envisioned. The patriots wanted warfare, not mystery, the leaders tradition, not mystery!

Nicodemus had no sooner confessed that rabbi had come from God than rabbi became his instructor. And Nicodemus discovered that he had no spiritual experience to process teacher's remarkable instruction. Israel as a political body, Nicodemus could grasp; or as a religious nation; and Jesus as a New prophet of the Old Mosaic order. But rabbi determined to

institute an entirely new spiritual order, where the commonest
Jew had equal rights with the highest priest, where the
Sanhedrin members had no advantage over the lepers, where
people excelled temples and where everyone had to be *reborn*
to enter the kingdom. Nicodemus blanched at every revolutionary concept, especially at the idea of being reborn.
Whatever our persuasions, however, rabbi had no intention of
building a stratified kingdom. *Everyone* would be renewed
from above, even those leading Israel, even those looking for
the redemption of Israel!

The unvarying emphasis on forgiveness remained the heart
of rabbi's ministry. Give him his due...he never deviated from
it. He repeatedly stressed that our hope of national renewal
began with personal forgiveness!

There was something else in his teaching I only gradually
understood: signs that to Nicodemus and us portended the messianic kingdom, to Jesus proved only a reference to something
greater, deeper and spiritual: himself as the final, ultimate proof
of his claims, with signs important only because *he* offered
them. They *reflected*, not identified his being! And...most im-
portantly...he himself was the sign the leaders never accepted,
the source of constant turmoil throughout his ministry! He
refused to diminish it by associating it with any other cause or
endeavor. He magnified it by insinuating that all other
problems found their solutions in him!

Rabbi revealed the kingdom's true nature and called
Nicodemus to accept it. Unflattered by the attention of such a
renowned man and August body, whose approval would
guarantee his acceptance in Israel, he disconcertingly dis-
tanced himself from everyone he met, including those
accustomed to deference from all.

Everything in his ministry flowed from that first interview.
He quickly established himself as a miracle worker, but only as
acts of mercy, never for political or personal gain—not even
demanding discipleship from those helped!

I became intensely aware of our divergent perspectives at
our second Passover together. Healing the lame man revealed
rabbi as a man aware of God at a level no one else ever
reached; in concepts not discussed by priest, prophet or
flaming insurrectionist. The shock reverberated through me,
and I realized I may have mistaken the man! But, not willing

to quickly surrender my hopes, and his fulfillment of them, I remained among the disciples-at -large.

On our return to Galilee came controversies, miracles and teachings, all of which focused on healing disease, forgiving sins and converting sinners—without a single criticism of the Roman occupation that made life miserable, burdened us with onerous taxes, stole our self-esteem and made us servants of whatever imposition Roman troopers made. He effectively doused my messianic hopes with frigid finality—which I kept rewarming to life by adamant insistence on their necessity! I began to wonder how I could have committed myself to his plainly unmilitary and nonpolitical ministry.

Then rabbi left the multitude, climbed the hills to pray and next day called the crowd to him and completed his inner circle. Hoping to be chosen, but fearing my caution and reserve disqualified me, I soared when rabbi called my name: me, a Judean chosen among all the Galileans present! My dreams had come true, eroding my misgivings. Surely he would now tailor his ministry to more carefully reflect Israel's political expectations.

However, even there it occurred to me: a warrior-king wouldn't pick his closest associates by praying the night through over the choices. Warrior prowess, political insights and connections among the leadership would be sought. And what chieftain would make rabbi's choices if he intended to fight Rome—with myself alone experienced in guerilla warfare?

In his sermon from the mountain teacher considered blessed what I considered remarkably pacific, lacking force, and remarkably spiritual, lacking military application. With everyone else, I supported their general intention, while ridiculing their practical use. I mourned only our political slavery; I felt poor only because Rome overtaxed us, I hungered only for the demolition of Roman power; I understood peacemaking only as the absence of warfare, achieved by killing and maiming and imprisoning more of the enemy than he of us; I accepted wrath only on those bereft of righteousness, not persecution for being righteous.

Other than these objections, nothing in the beatitudes particularly bothered me.

Actually, their distinct lack of militance distressed me. I missed the clashing of sabers, the pounding of swords against leather shields. My class wanted revolution, not peace talks;

swords, not plowshares! His miracles hinted of battle with invisible forces in invisible worlds, while I wanted very visible
legions banished from Israel! I could never reconcile the difference between David's military victories and rabbi's
miracles.

The entire sermon disappointed anyone seeking political
and military redress of the wrongs plaguing our society. I
didn't want to hear such irrelevant teachings as to which law
was greater; rabbis disputed that endlessly. I didn't want to
hear about forgiving enemies; I wanted them eliminated.
When rabbi talked about adultery in the mind, I felt that,
human nature being what it was, eliminating actual adultery
posed enough difficulty. Because women meant nothing to
him, must he punish everyone else?

And divorce being wrong? How could he overturn 1500
years of tradition? If Moses was good enough for all previous
generations, why change now? And turning the other cheek?
Going two miles for Roman soldier who impressed into service
for one hateful mile? Not in my lifetime!

We weren't so concerned about clearing our life of wrongs
as righting the many wrongs perpetrated by the legions! We
figured to redress our wrongs after liberating Israel. We
couldn't imagine more harm could be done trying to oust Rome
than ignoring their presence. But rabbi disagreed!

Another defining moment in my disaffection occurred on
what the disciples came to call the "long day" of rabbi's
ministry. It proved definitive to me, but in a way different from
the eleven. Rabbi had in that magnificent crowd many willing
to be recruited—including the leadership—needing only
specific instruction to abandon career, home and life for him.
And, I couldn't believe it even then, he talked in parables—
stories no one could apply to the historic situation! We finally
asked him in private why he used that method when people
needed clear, unquestionable dialogue. If he intended to encourage us, he only discouraged me more by assuring us that
perspicacity belonged to us, not to the crowds. If so, why did
we lack it? He even assured us how fortunate we were to hear
obscure teaching! Whatever the promised benefits of his ob-
fuscation, and our ultimate clarification, it seethed with
unexplained discrepancies. Even explaining in private surfaced
as many questions as he resolved, with more damned riddles as

explanations! Why use that method when it unsettled the very people he needed to impress?

His intimidation of us complete, however, when he asked if we understood, like dumb beasts we nodded, and he went on to add perplexing statements about old and new treasure. When we had no treasure at all as far as I could tell! *What a strange man*, I thought to myself.

I began to think I must have more in common with the Pharisees than with rabbi, for I never understood the parables. What was worse, I detected no scent of political activism and military recruitment in them. The only reference to war was the parable of the king going to war with ten thousand men— which he offered much later. And what did he mean to imply by it if not that we, as Jews with a smaller army, should make peace with the more powerful Romans? NOT what I wanted to hear!

The night after the "longest day," we sailed eastward across Gennesaret into the fiercest storm I had experienced to that time. We awakened rabbi and he instantly calmed both winds and waves. He expressed complete power over the forces of nature, the spirit world, illness, paralysis and leprosy but never exercised power against Rome! He had all the power Israel needed against the legions but used it only against winds, waves and demons! He had everything...except the will to *use* it against our oppressors!

Then came the definitive event, the third of three tours of Galilee that I hoped would eliminate all the questions I had accumulated, remove all the doubts I harbored, and arouse in me the faith I still wanted, but found increasingly impossible to hold! He seemed to suddenly be aware of the coming kingdom. And delighting the Twelve, gave us his authority over unclean spirits, sickness and disease. We would be extensions of himself!

If he didn't have bigger plans in mind, why order us on a nationwide preaching campaign preparing for his later arrival? We went. We persevered. We succeeded beyond our wildest expectations. We returned, suffused with hope for a long-sought kingdom!

To no avail. After feeding 5000 increasingly excited men and their equally enthused families, he refused their acclamation as king—the very goal I wanted achieved, which would repay all my dissatisfactions, remove my contempt and restore my hope! Never did rabbi prove less qualified as our leader!

That crushing blow led me to despise him, whatever he said or did thereafter. I had been over two years coming to my conclusion, hoping I'd never reach it. But when I had I wouldn't budge from it: rabbi couldn't be trusted to fulfill my goals! When, the next day, he tried to convince me and the vast crowd that followed him to Capernaum from the eastern shore, that we should eat his body and drink his blood, I turned away in loathing. How reprehensible to those who saw Messiah as a charismatic warrior leading, not a mystical figure sharing his inner being with the people!

If the eleven, in that synagogue, reverted to a past they were convinced gave hope to their future, I looked there and saw *nothing* but discomfiting discouragements and disappointments! He had previously demoralized my hope. In the synagogue he devastated it! The sun would rise from the Great Sea before I ever believed in him again!

I went through the motions this past year, feeling no love for rabbi and fighting a growing revulsion of him and his boot–licking Galileans. I found myself finding fault with everything he did or said, however the others savored it. I favored the leaders since I knew rabbi had forfeited his chance to be our national leader. Back to the constituted leaders the people should turn, away from the false prophet who had arrogated their place. The determination grew in me: find a way to meet with the leaders so they can force rabbi to his senses!

When we failed to exorcise the demon at the foot of the mountain, I sardonically questioned, *why shouldn't we fail him, since he's so often failed me?*

I pacified my disappointment when rabbi defended an unknown preacher who exorcised demons in his name by sarcastically saying that *someone* should make use of his power since he obviously wouldn't—and wouldn't let any of the Twelve!

He talked religious theory when we needed political and military planning! He talked forgiveness when we needed our rights! He lectured on brotherly responsibility while I sought instructions for killing Romans. He didn't know the importance of discussing problems the people faced and wanted resolved. *Get to the important issues, rabbi*, I kept muttering to myself, *that people feel are essential to their daily lives, not what you feel relates to some heavenly experience.* I knew rabbi was no politician or soldier!

When he later sent seventy of us out, most of them without our credentials, all returned tumultuously successful. According to his custom, teacher subordinated our great achievement to having our names written in Heaven. How having our names written in Heaven related to establishing God's kingdom on earth, they wondered, he never said, and I no longer cared!

To show how alienated from the eleven I had become, they *sought* instruction from rabbi on prayer. Personally, I'd had enough lessons on it, and enough time spent watching and waiting while he prayed. In reply, he told the story about the friend at midnight. It surfaced an impression I hadn't really considered before: rabbi had a genius for storytelling I'm quite sure is unique in history. And to find spiritual applications in everyday events is still astonishing to me. Why didn't he use that genius to tell stories of David's battles with the Philistines, or of the night the angel destroyed 185,000 Assyrians outside Jerusalem? Why did every story have a religious, not a militant point!

Other teachings followed, so many I can't specify, each with some spiritual emphasis I didn't remember and forgot as quickly as possible.

Never, whether taking about money, the rich fool, the parables of workers and vineyards, healings in the synagogue or his identity, did rabbi fail to divide the crowd for and against him, and embitter the leadership until they wanted him dead! I considered all of this alien to Messiah's work, which we expected would *unite* Israel for an attack on Rome, not divide Israel over every issue he raised!

He never compromised his approach, give him that. He had committed himself to being a teacher in Israel, and would be nothing but. I had hoped for much more. I got much less.

RETROSPECT

Since I finally and unsparingly despised everything rabbi became, I still can't agree with his emphasis on religious, moral and spiritual themes. That heartlessly violated my perception of Messiah's work and David's kingdom!

I can only grudgingly admit that Jesus of Nazareth proved perfectly consistent. He never saw Rome as a threat; he held its servants in high regard and demanded Jewish submission to its laws and taxes.

His appeal was also consistently deliberative and contemplative, not impulsive and inflammatory. His teaching never failed to provoke thought, concentration and insight; and never struck with the thunder and lightning patriots wanted or with the revolutionary summons insurrectionists sought.

Still, give rabbi credit—and I know this is the result of his consistent religious emphasis—large crowds never impressed him. While other teachers would take advantage and stress rewards coming to the faithful, he warned of the cost to be paid serving him. While other leaders lured followers by the *promise* of great benefits, he courageously demanded self-denial as the prior condition to following him.

The first time he actually made that demand was after the eleven confessed him as the Son of God. Had he made it earlier, I would have walked! By that time I already had mentally, so I disgustedly grunted. Somehow, the teaching got a more positive response from the eleven. How they continued to believe in rabbi, despite as many reasons to deny him, I'll never know. Some people are just more gullible!

I'm still tormented by the contrast between rabbi's convincing humility and incredible claims. He could be so seriously humble in behavior and life and so boastful about God as his father and himself as the center of God's kingdom! I can't deny them as so much hypocrisy. I wish I could. Even now I admit he was filled with such grace that no one, not even I, objected to his life. I differed only in methodology.

But didn't he have to be an unbalanced personality to have such contradictory traits in his personality? Even his family once feared for his sanity. And more than once both leaders and crowds ascribed his powers to demons. That surely has to be it...that has to be it: his great passion for God drove him mad!

That's my conviction, and I'm sticking to it. For I refuse to consider the alternative: that he could simultaneously be as humble as he asserted and as great as he claimed precisely because he was the Messiah others thought and the Son of God the disciples confessed! I cannot tolerate such a supposition. It contradicts all my perceptions. It denounces all my dreams. It damns my soul!

ALIENATION OF THE LEADERSHIP

This past Monday all possibility of reconciliation vanished, and I rejoiced in my agreement with the Sanhedrin. Rabbi came raging into town and attacked, not Fortress Antonia, but the sacred precincts. When he could have declared war on Rome, he declared it on what he called the tainted religious life of corrupt religious leaders. He had to know—with this being the second time in three years, and at the same time of the year—the Sadducees wouldn't tolerate his interference!

Earlier in his ministry I stood aghast with awe at his temple tantrum; now I stood aghast with rage. He had acquired no appreciation of their position, investment and responsibility for maintaining peace in the temple, where even a *hint* of violence would bring the legionnaires.

As I watched, suddenly I understood: *it's always been a dispute over rights. At the time of the first cleansing, and ever after, an incessant point of rancor—his revolutionary authority colliding with their vested traditionalism; he acting from inner dictates, they from the centuries!*

Why hadn't I seen it at the first? They endlessly disputed the right to rule Israel! "What is your authority?", they asked when Jesus cleansed the temple at the beginning and their question when he cleansed the temple this week! The *source* of their three year contention, they camped like opposing armies around that issue. Who had the authority to represent God to Israel? Who was responsible for our national and religious life?

Within weeks of his first temple appearance rabbi had established ministry models which declared *his* authority, each disputed by leaders defending *theirs*. He considered his a breakthrough into an unlimited future, they a menace to a closed past. He uncovered each in different figures, but always as replications of his original claim, sometimes more clearly, or less distinct, but always relevant to his initial intent. In each case the leaders, far more intuitive than the rest of us, sensed their poverty in his prosperity and their demise in his success. To preserve their position, they initiated the opposition that ultimately led me to betrayal and rabbi to Pilate's Judgment Hall.

EXORCISMS

His first exorcism in Capernaum stimulated rave notices throughout Galilee, and thousands filled the roads seeking him. Caught by surprise, the leaders planned to intervene if it happened again. Rabbi obliged them during our second tour of Galilee, and they attributed his power to Beelzebub. We gasped in disbelief. How could they conjecture a Satanic force for such a godly act? Perhaps rabbi needed to explain how he intended to use his power, but he shouldn't have to *defend* an exorcism. That spoke for itself!

Even then, however, I instinctively realized that his autocratic style had created a problem he didn't intend to resolve. He never consulted constituted authority for their opinion, or made an effort to involve them, or took them into his confidence or explained anything. Indeed, his consistent *practice* of authority destroyed all principles of compromise! What alternative but suspicion did they have? Why should he be right and those *already* in authority wrong?

However, while rabbi consistently ignored acclamations as the son of David, and proved oblivious to personal social slights, he took pointed exception when accused of collusion with Beelzebub! That never failed to offend and rouse him. And *that* never failed to impress the Twelve.

I'm still convinced, however, that simply claiming God as his source would have eliminated many of the questions he allowed to fester into acrimony. Israel had a tradition of prophets possessing astonishing powers they always ascribed to God! Who was this new teacher who healed, exorcised and taught from sources within himself?

Their suspicions still hadn't been eliminated at the end of the second tour of Galilee months later. His earlier warning had made no impact on them, while they remained satisfied with their earlier accusation. An impasse had already been reached, and they would shortly be snorting across the landscape like red-eyed bulls ready to gore the competition!

To stop the rush into confrontation I sensed the need for mediation. Sheathe their swords, enter into dialogue and let arbitrators find the common ground that surely existed between them, since they all had Israel's welfare at heart.

Without it, given the extremism on both sides, strident accusations could easily become physical violence. Rabbi could surely see the danger, since death threats had already been made. He owed it to himself to have a sit-down, air-clearing, confidence-building conference with those who could guarantee him nation-wide acceptance. If he not only refused to pay the king his shilling, but ordered the king to abdicate so he could ascend the throne, understanding wouldn't increase!

MOSES AND TRADITION

After being embarrassed in the first Passover, the Pharisees followed rabbi's every move. Within six months he attracted enough attention and enjoyed enough popularity that John's own disciples took umbrage. The leaders began to watch him even more critically.

Herod Antipas then arrested John, and unrelenting scrutiny shifted to Jesus. To defuse antagonism, he left for Galilee.

When his Galilean ministry began, he seemed an obedient servant of Moses "...offer the sacrifices that Moses commanded for your cleansing...", he ordered the leper. But he as quickly disregarded, then contradicted Moses and the fathers.

First came the healing of the paralytic, with rabbi's cavalier pronouncement of the man's *forgiveness*. Everyone shuddered at his effrontery! Even if he proved forgiveness by healing the man, that remained the domain of the sacrificial system, with authorized priests ordained to perform the necessary functions! God had zealously guarded their prerogative, even slaying Kohath and his conspirators when they objected. Why did teacher act so arbitrarily, outside all existing authority? Why have the temple at all if he could forgive with a word?

Or did he have no further use of the temple? Why then pay the half shekel to maintain it? Had he become so insane with ambition and egotism that he dared see himself as its replacement? Surely he had to be stopped before he ruined us!

And I stopped him! But—now that I have—are we any safer?

Then came criticism over his refusal to observe the fasts
that tradition prescribed and our people had faithfully obeyed.

He strongly defended his position, offering himself as the
reason! What an interesting man I followed, I said at the time.
I very soon thought him something different from *interesting*!

That controversy had hardly settled when rabbi intentionally provoked violent confrontation at our second Passover.
Naturally, it occurred in the temple and, naturally, on a
Sabbath! Would he have healed the lame man had he known it
would surface an issue that remained bitterly contested six
months later?

Saying more than I felt the occasion demanded—it would
have been better to claim it after accumulating overwhelming
evidence—he defended the miracle as an example of God's
continuing activity in him as God's Son.

Their heated death threat followed; a warning for him to
become more accommodating!

The disciples were equally amazed at his claims and terrified by the ferment they aroused. A year into his ministry,
and the leaders wanted him dead! If he didn't cool the
rhetoric, let tempers settle, re-assess each other's position, and
find common ground, he soon would be! They had the resources, he the vulnerability!

After this came the controversy over signs, at the beginning
of our second tour of Galilee. After rabbi and the leaders
emptied their respective ink wells throwing insults about
origins and alliances, they asked him for a sign. I impulsively
considered them impertinent. Having failed to identify rabbi
with Satan in the popular imagination, they seemed determined
on provocation.

The *more* I pondered, and the less enchanted I became with
rabbi, the *more* logical I considered their request—indeed a
commendable effort to re-establish dialogue given the preju-
dicial charges exchanged between them. Maybe their initiative
would win rabbi over. This was a vain hope, however; intolerant of interrogation, he declared that only an evil and
adulterous generation demanded signs!

That seemed inconsistent. He had become famous by offering signs, but felt offended when they were requested. He
performed signs at his leisure, for numerous people, but
wouldn't perform one to pacify the leaders and to enlist their

support, diminish their suspicions and put an end to the constant bickering! Hadn't God offered Aaron's budding rod for just that reason?

Of course their demands for signs grew with their opposition. On our brief visit to Dalmanutha, both Pharisees and Sadducees approached rabbi with the usual request. The addition of *Sadducees* alarmed the eleven. Sadducees in the far north of Galilee? What danger had rabbi unintentionally engendered?

However ominous to the eleven, I saw their appearance as an opportunity for dialogue. Rabbi could master one group, but could he overcome their alliance? And if he attracted opposition from the Sadducees, though he restricted his ministry to Galilee, not threatening the temple, had the time finally come to finally seek reconciliation, admitting how irreconcilable he had become? Their junction represented a last-ditch effort to establish peace with teacher—or at least an understanding. It might even elicit their support if he offered proof of his prophetic calling.

Jesus buried his refusal in concrete: signs aplenty as acts of mercy, but not one as proof on demand by a leadership not convinced by any sign or teaching previously given! Indeed, saying that the leaders could read the sky, but not the times, he curtly predicted no sign but Jonah's.

Rabbi had become intentionally obnoxious, habitually irritating the authorities, baiting instead of co-operating with them and violating rather than submitting to Moses. I adamantly objected to his endles provocations. Always afterward, in one event after another, he knowingly deepened the rift between himself and the leaders that his actions in Jerusalem had initially created. And I concluded that he was not only much less than I had supposed but also much less than he claimed! As we followed rabbi out that day, I looked at the leaders and shook my head in what I hoped they saw as disappointment with him, then left in dismay, absolutely convinced that I had to force a compromise!

SYNAGOGUES

Rabbi went into the synagogues and usurped what they had ruled for generations. He saw a man there with a withered hand. With the rulers glowering, waiting for him to do something illegal, and the people squirming in expectation, wanting him to, he did!

Rabbi had everyone look at the shrunken arm the man carried across his chest like a chicken's wing. Then commanded him to extend it! Impossible! But he did it, tentatively at first, then robustly. It fleshed out, mature fingernails appeared, he twirled his restored arm around, gawked at it, smiled, started to cry and fell sobbing before the seated teacher.

Adoration burst like a meteor shower, while the leaders hovered in rage without recourse; how could they fault such a miracle? But outside Herodians and Pharisees talked together, heads down, glancing angrily at Jesus, obviously plotting against him. Later that day we learned they wanted him dead. Now...not one, not two, but all three major groups in Israel opposed and wanted him dead! And not only in Judea, which he could avoid, but in Galilee, where he lived! He had to rethink his strategy. It was suicidal to continue using their own synagogues as instruments of confrontation. Why be the one man in his whole generation to brazenly disregard their statutes, knowing it would force natural enemies into an alliance against his incendiary threat!

THIS WEEK'S CONTROVERSIES

The old authority issue resurfaced: they questioned his; he refused theirs. Always having the last word, he aimed the Parable of the Vineyard at them. I never saw them so incensed! For he vehemently guaranteed their ejection from the kingdom! They knew it, we knew it, no one could misunderstand it! Only public opinion prevented his immediate seizure and death!

When he referred to the Psalms as proof of his divine Sonship, they finally discovered what had become clear to me eighteen months before: rabbi would always have more to ask than they could answer; and more to say than they could master. By claiming a special relationship with God he set himself apart from everyone!

We all found him too powerful, adamant, flawless and irresistible! Why didn't I find him the Anointed of God?

Nothing prepared me for his bruising verbal flagellation of the religious bureaucracy. It terrified me. *Had I waited too long to secure rabbi's arrest?*, I wondered. Only the knowledge of our arrangement restrained them—but premonition shouted that when they had him in their power, their aggressive, aggregate wrath would show no mercy, having been shown none by him. Having been so searingly disheartened by rabbi, I shared their animosity—though I still trusted their pacific intentions!

Everyone finally understood: as an immoderate absolutist, rabbi demanded the alteration of existing institutions to his design. He wouldn't prune the old to make it more fruitful; or graft new to the old to make it serviceable; or repair the defective in Judaism or modify its character to meet changing societal needs. He would destroy everything already built, the present leadership with it, then establish himself in their place. No doubt existed in my mind: he intended to replace what Moses had administered for 1500 years. Someone had to stand in the breach for the sake of Israel, to eliminate the constant friction in the opposing sides and develop a consensus everyone could accept and support. For it was the nation, not the Messiah, or the religious leadership, that embodied the kingdom of God. The Messiah was important only if he retrieved Israelites from the dispersion, replanted them in their holy land and exalted them above the nations! Only then would he fulfill his destiny; not until!

RETROSPECT

As I reconsider, contradictory perceptions blind me. Both my appreciation of rabbi and my contempt of the leadership have soared in the past 12 hours. However much I've accused rabbi of discrepancies, he expressed a consistency amazingly true to his initial public appearances. In his earliest acts he forecast his subsequent ministry.

The pivotal interview with Nicodemus clearly revealed the religious basis of rabbi's life. We thought Nicodemus' arrival mysterious and portentous. "Why had *he* come?," we asked among ourselves. "Was it related to the temple cleansing?"

The fact that such a great man referred to our uncertified, unknown Galilean as *rabbi* underscored the obvious: rabbi had appeared from oblivion to become a sensation! Like the Sadducees, Nicodemus asked the source of his authority, but with a different motive. Nicodemus' question wasn't, "who gave you this authority," but, "what *kind* of authority did God give you, and for what purpose?" Perhaps his oblique inquiry meant, "Could you be the Messiah John promised?"

For my purposes, there also existed an unmentioned possibility in the question, which I hoped would be broached by the Sanhedrist—the fact that rabbi came from Galilee. That could only increase the unease in Jerusalem while it stimulated the northerners—and myself with them, in this case. Always a hotbed of warrior Messiahs, pretenders to the office regularly arose, recruited followers and led them in bloody clashes with the legionnaires. Was Jesus one of these?

What the establishment rabbi learned—what all who later related to rabbi learned—he would be disappointed if he hoped to bring Jesus under the protective wing of friendly Sanhedrin rabbi's. Our teacher would be as audaciously independent of the authorities as John,...and, as it turned out, as disastrously for both!

However, as I now berate myself: while I learned so much, and understood so little, so had Nicodemus. I listened to everything the teacher said, and to everything people said about him, until I was so confused I didn't know what to think—but so had Nicodemus! Should I have demanded more evidence than he, skilled leader that he was, unskilled layman that I was, with his intellectual superiority to me, with so much more to lose? His continuing faith in rabbi proved that lack of understanding didn't necessarily lead to disbelief. In Nicodemus the eleven found their model; in me the religious leadership discovered theirs.

And the fact that Jesus so naturally discussed issues prophets hadn't even approached, *strengthened* Nicodemus' trust in him. It proved that Jesus possessed much more than he revealed, though he revealed much! It all floored the man without spiritual peer in the Sanhedrin, as it increased his excitement over Jesus as a man! He concluded that Jesus of Nazareth's teaching was inexplicable because he was!

In the last few hours I've *begun* to understand how seriously wrong my perceptions about rabbi vis a vís the leadership have been. In one way, I wonder how my innocence could suffer such a fate at the hands of both parties I only wanted to reconcile. In another, however, if **only** I hadn't been so quick to condemn him and acquit them!

I wondered why he possessed inexplicable antipathy for them over every slight difference, ascribing dark motives to them. Now I know: he considered himself completely different from the leadership that had come to power by political machination and remained in power by political compromise. In rabbi's view, he and the Sanhedrin weren't two similar groups with equal but different rights, lovers quarreling, sometimes heatedly, more over details than substance—but wholly separate groups with convictions reflecting their opposite origins.

As time passed, and I discovered his real intent, I found I favored the aristocrats, for all their hypocrisies, to Jesus, with all his integrity. For they offered me more of what I had known while he offered only mystery!

I once thought rabbi solely responsible for the chasm of opposition opened between them. That he foreordained the conflict by his stubborn presence. If he had only *begun* differently with them, I reasoned, maybe the alienation would have been avoided, and he wouldn't have ended so tragically. Now I'm confident: nothing teacher could have done differently would have convinced them, for it was *he himself*, not a lack of signs or concessions, that enraged them. Being Him posed a threat to Them! Like pegs sticking through a board, rabbi's originality got hammered. For all my questions, I've never had any doubts about the clarity of his singularity! And nothing short of surrendering it would have shrunk the distance that his originality and their conformity inevitably surfaced! Since they couldn't conquer his innovation with their tradition, they despised *him*. Since he couldn't be another, and they wouldn't be, his presence offered a menace they wanted removed!

Could I have been so blind...it was the *person* the leaders hated and I rejected. We used his teachings, miracles, obscurity and claims as excuses, to hide our fear and loathing of

HIM! He created faith in *himself* and made *himself* the essence of every lesson, sermon and miracle, the deity other human vessels only represented, the Word of God others merely communicated—the heart, soul and center of God's kingdom!

As I ponder it now: isn't that why he always proved too powerful, too immune, too unconquerable, too inviolate for everyone he faced, everyone who opposed him, everyone who loved him? For whoever claimed authority in Israel, he had the influence!

I'm ashamed to admit that I allied myself with them, not with him. They rebelled against him, despite good reasons to submit, and I lost faith in him, despite good reasons to believe.

I never saw an *original* person until I saw rabbi! His daring staggered me, and still does. But if he is *that* original, is that why none of us understood him? Indeed, who will ever understand him? *No one in our generation, certainly!* I guess those to come will have to take all of him they can by knowledge, and the rest of him by faith! I couldn't; and that's my mistake!

I realize also that the most intractable opponents of new methods and new teachings are those not only *accustomed* to old methods and teachings, but those determined to *retain* them! For where originality requires purpose, custom requires only existence! The guardians of orthodoxy, not rabbi, created the heresy: the traditionalists who vilified innovation; the ceremonialists who denigrated substance. Indeed, I now see that they demanded the right to filter everything rabbi said through their authority, however it expressed itself. *That* eliminated change. And that had been the result of every prophet's ministry. Has Israel learned nothing from its past, guaranteeing a repetition of the mistakes that brought disaster on our fathers, and will inflict more on us?

I once criticized teacher for his hard-driving expectation of obedience. The leaders might be *led*, I thought, but would never be *driven* to follow him. But now I know: their stubborn personal interests hardened them against submission to anyone, let alone someone so singular! Someone only *somewhat* different would have estranged and threatened them; our rabbi's self-designed spontaneity inevitably alienated them.

As the possibility of compromise disappeared, I thought that conspiring with the Sanhedrin—those I felt possessed ultimate authority in Israel—offered the only solution. And, bitter as I feel about it—even rabbi now understands: their vested position guaranteed that *no one* could so publicly and continually embarrass them without eventually experiencing their revenge. What rabbi began in the temple three years ago has concluded in Caiaphas' palace: they, not he, will rule this land!

Why then am I so unhappy? Why can't I convince myself that the *results* have equaled the sincerity of my intentions? Why, having sided with the leaders, do I now consider their reactions to rabbi the blighting ignorance he called it?

I still have no explanation for him. I wish I did; it would quiet the relentless torment I feel having betrayed him. I do know this: whatever depths he uncovered, greater unsounded depths remained in him, untouched and possibly entirely unfathomable. He may have revealed less to spare us further perplexity! Maybe the best thing he ever did was to shield us from what would otherwise have driven us insane! For only a person who *was* all he *claimed* could contain his mystery without going mad with delusions of grandeur.

His perspectives still hopelessly confuse me. I matured in Moses through forms, symbols and ceremonies, and journeyed into bewilderment through rabbi's foundational originality! Yet what to conclude about each I find impossible to say. I can say that 3 years under rabbi intellectually and religiously stretched me more than 30 under Moses!

In the end, both rabbi and the Sanhedrin proved false to me: the leaders because they protected their privileges, rabbi because he saved souls. I had learned to expect political compromise with Rome from the leaders, since their vested interest demanded co-operation with the Tiber. But what did Caesar offer rabbi but more of the same bondage we had suffered since Pompey captured Jerusalem? Forgive the leaders; they're just politicians, after all. But hold rabbi responsible; he could have made the difference and refused! And while I disrespect the leaders for the compromises that led to our national impoverishment, I despise rabbi for not using his powers to remove it. He deserves to be punished for refusing his destiny, when he alone of all those in our generation could have *risen* to it! Why didn't he, with all his influence, kindle into inferno the fire waiting only the oxygen of some charismatic leader's breath?

Jesus of Nazareth assassinated my soaring hopes, and I'm embittered past the degree of my previous hope! If I've betrayed him, he betrayed me first. If I've effectively assassinated him by conspiring with the leaders, he first destroyed my dreams! I swear by the temple above this canyon that my love for Israel has flourished as my respect for rabbi has diminished. I still believe all the promises made to our prophets. God will yet send the man to regain what our forefathers lost when they invited the Romans to settle irreconcilable differences among our people; to assume the responsibility the Sanhedrin won't and rabbi wouldn't. Responsibility must be assumed: Israel shall survive; Jerusalem shall remain; the temple shall STAND!

I *think* I made the right decision. I'm *sure* I made the right decision. I *know* I made the right decision. Rabbi, why can't you understand that decision? Please understand my motive, rabbi, you who saw everyone's motive so clearly. And judge me by my *motive*, not by the results of my action! I did it because I loved my people; because I felt you betrayed my people!

When we both deserve to live, not die, **why** am I here, ready to die, and you as surely condemned to die? How could our dreams vanish into the death wish I now express and the death sentence you now experience?

PART III

BETRAYAL
AND
REGRET

THE SNARE IS SET

Visitors to Bethany from Jerusalem brought astounding news: of the people's rabid speculation about rabbi and his inevitable public appearance in the city; that Lazarus could be assassinated for his association with rabbi; that the authorities had ordered everyone to report rabbi's location so he could be arrested.

So the authorities have finally decided made an all-out effort against rabbi's influence, I pondered! *His intransigence has made it inevitable.*

While the intelligence created unease in the disciples, inflicting a finality they couldn't face, it supplied me a definition I couldn't deny—and like sparks to combustion, my determination flared! The opportune time had come to execute my long-developing plan to reconcile him and the leaders. I would force arbitration that soothed them and salvaged him.

Questions clouded the decision, however: should I gamble my life by urging teacher to consult with them? But why bother? He had never taken anyone's advice about anything and certainly wouldn't take mine about co-operating with the authorities. Should I contact Nicodemus or Joseph with my plan? But they would immediately refer my request to Jesus—and would I ever be tongue-lashed, and maybe evicted from the group! I certainly couldn't talk to the other disciples, because they would brand me a traitor. I heartened myself with the assurance that I, like all great men, had to stand alone in the crisis. And if I achieved my goal, even the dreamy-eyed Galileans would extol me!

I committed myself to approaching a Sanhedrin member! Which in itself posed uncertainties. Would they despise me as a disciple of the man they hated? Would they agree to my terms? What would I offer as a rationale?

Whatever my questions, I had no further use for rabbi. I had listened to his vexatious circumlocution for three years without getting any clearer about or any closer to the kingdom Israel needed. As I saw it, so long as rabbi lived, it would be more of the same advance and retreat, progress and reversion he had always followed.

I wanted to breathe my own air after walking in his dust. If I couldn't force him into accountability to the Sanhedrin, I was finished, literally with him and figuratively with personal involvement in the kingdom of God. I wouldn't waste my life following a leader who always got suspended between dreams and reality.

Ironically, rabbi himself provided the catalyst! Simon strained the usual Sabbath rules to express his appreciation of rabbi at a splendid feast. Everyone happily participated, and people constantly arrived to see Lazarus and teacher, who seemed unusually insouciant.

Then Mary entered, broke the jar and splashed rabbi's head and feet with her perfume. The cascading bouquet at first stunned, then angered me. Here we were, a nearly-penniless group, and she wasted the delicate fragrance on rabbi's extremities — especially inappropriate when he knew the precariousness of our financial condition and the limitations under which we labored! I struggled daily with the impossible challenge of funding his generosity. And now, with the burden of alms always heavier at Passover, and Jesus never meeting a beggar he didn't want to help, Mary's wild zeal further imperiled us!

I instinctively blurted my objection. And though I considered *waste* the proper word, if I had taken time to think, I would have chosen something less confrontational. The *word* certainly shocked his devotees, who figured nothing given their precious Master could be wasted.

In that instant I couldn't take any more of what I had always considered his misuse of resources. I had watched him waste money on others and choked down my irritation. As he tolerated waste on himself, my accumulated fury surfaced!

Deadly silence supervened. Had I wished, I could have removed the embarrassment by saying I would have felt differently had rabbi established the kingdom he always promised; had we now sat on those twelve thrones he predicted; had we seen *any* of the "hundred times over" he foresaw! Then nothing anyone did for him would have been *excessive*, and *I* would have *prompted* it and provided funds from our treasury.

But why bother to say the obvious that he would harshly condemn?

Financial constraints alone forced the evaluation! If others ascribed my expostulation to greed, I knew by then I had to provide for myself, or would fall victim to the same irresponsibility that consumed Jesus of Nazareth. If my appreciation of money increased as my faith in him declined, he changed my values. As with any deteriorating relationship, those involved take from it what they *can* before it collapses! Since I had no further connection to teacher, I should at least have access to the common purse for my own good! That represented merely a small measure of revenge against him.

Interestingly, and I'm sure they'll never make this public, other disciples also felt the impropriety, adopted my indignation and vocally questioned the anointing. If my criticism seemed an indictment of *waste* on him compared to the *need* others felt, I hadn't been alone in making it.

However, teacher took exception to our exception by defending her. More accurately, as he sat up and put his bare feet on the floor, with all eyes turned to him, I felt he looked daggers at *me*! To this hour I can feel them ripping through me!

I wanted to hide under the pillow! In the flickering lamps, their faces showing agitation, whether at me or at Jesus, everyone hushed. And, as he spoke of Mary's *wonderful* act, everyone but myself changed sides and admitted that, if Jesus approved, they had no objection.

I seethed as the rest returned to previous conversations, ignoring me, making me a pariah—as if I alone had objected! Had I not feared attack by the disciples, I would have bolted immediately and contacted the authorities. Instead I swallowed my pride and nourished a mushrooming antipathy for a rabbi who, in defending a woman against me, proved himself unworthy of my confidence! I WOULD SHOW HIM!

The inspirational moment had seized me and built a forge from the particles of resentment hanging in my mind; I would *batter* rabbi to an awareness of his true mission. I *determined* to turn him over as I had earlier *planned to!* If by some miracle he *were* Messiah, maybe finding himself under arrest would rouse his instinct for self-preservation.

I looked for the opportunity!

Little did I know that rabbi would again provide it when he entered Jerusalem this past Sunday. As never before, he openly

scorned the leadership. As never before he openly accepted the
bedlam that hovered chaotically around him. Lost in loathing
for the way he treated me, for the way he made, then broke
promises, and for things I'd forgotten but resurfaced mentally, I
shivered with fury. *Why make fools of yourselves?*, I cursed as
cheering rolled.

Then, as the road fell from the crown of Olivet, rabbi did
what *I would have predicted*, but which no one else expected:
he killed the flourishing efflorescence in the crowd by *condemning Jerusalem!* With the capital beyond his for the taking,
and he could have ridden in, even on that stupid donkey, and
recruited the whole population, and the leaders couldn't have
lifted a hand; when he could have destroyed my intention to
have him arrested—for who could defame the idol of the
hour?—he snatched defeat from the jaws of victory, defying
the decision that clamored, that beseeched, that begged, that
shouted to be made!

I *KNEW* he would do something outrageous.

When we entered the city, tumult again occurred, with
rabbi the focus. Word passed mouth to mouth: "Jesus of
Nazareth is here," and crowds jammed the narrow streets.
Only by pushing forward a little at a time did we gain the
temple. There the Pharisees naturally condemned and rabbi
naturally justified the shrill shouts of children. I thought it appropriate: he refused to rule adults, but made himself king of
the cradle!

The day's activities finally ended around evening sacrifice,
and we went in different directions, most of them by two's or
three's, but I alone, for work that no one else must know.
Alone, because *no other man* in the disciple band had the
sagacity to see the apocalypse rabbi's misguided idealism fore-
shadowed.

Anxiety, hope and dread convulsed me as I walked through
the temple to the offices of the chief priests. The plan that had
seemed so right suddenly seemed so unlikely now that I had to
implement it! Still, while afraid to act, I was more afraid to
refrain! I hadn't come to my conclusion without turbulent
soul-searching, calculating the possible cost against the incredible gains—now afraid; now fearless; now depressed, now
exultant! If I looked ahead, alarming portents terrified me. If

I looked behind, contempt suffused me. I couldn't go on as I had for the past three years, rabbi no closer to his goals, me no closer to mine. With this decision, I would fulfill or shatter my future!

He had to compromise with the leadership, and I could effect that by having him arrested and examined in private. Only then would he necessarily realize his errors and, under the threat of death if he didn't comply, adopt a collegial approach with the aristocracy.

Still, I dreaded the consequences if rabbi fought instead of surrendering when arrested—he possessed awesome powers! Where would I be then, open to his vengeance and the revenge of the eleven? And what if the leadership refused me, thinking it impossible that a member of his own group would betray him? But I would take pains to clarify: it wasn't a betrayal; it was simply a warning for rabbi, a desperate act to save him from what had become a self-imposed suicide mission. Now that the authorities had gone public with their demand to have him arrested, how long until he was? Why not have someone negotiate their differences, giving the leaders what they wanted and Jesus what he needed, awakening both to the necessity of compromise before violence erupted between them? Rabbi could continue as a great teacher and healer and they as the certified authorities whose presence he had ignored, whose position he had denigrated, whose influence he had diminished.

I could do that! I could be instrumental in effecting a reconciliation between the most powerful man I'd ever seen and the most powerful men in Israel!

I couldn't imagine they wouldn't welcome me. We had often heard—via Nicodemus—that the leaders constantly discussed ways to reach rabbi: talking to him, scheming against him, warning others about him—with no success. Surely they would be pleased that, just when it seemed their nemesis might again elude them, I would appear and arrange rabbi's *availability* for capture.

I underestimated their response by half! They couldn't believe their good fortune! What burgeoning satisfaction I felt as they vied with each other extolling my bravery and sagacity. Here I was, a commoner being treated like royalty by the aristocracy, when the common rabbi had treated me like a footstool!

Annas nodded enthusiastically when I announced I didn't
want vengeance against rabbi. Our goals were similar, he
assured me. Like myself, they had serious questions about the
rabbi's intentions. Though they hated to interfere with such a
popular figure, they had decided to arrest and *question*—I remember that word well—him and persuade him to re-direct his
energies to *save* Israel, not plunge her into disaster. My very
intention! I couldn't believe how generous they were, how
clearly selfless their motives and methods, how pacific their intentions. They wanted to reach an agreement with teacher, not
harm him. *If he had only consulted these fine men earlier*, I
thought, *what problems he could have avoided*! Changes had
to come in Israel's religious life, the leaders agreed. But not
change as rabbi envisioned it, for he demanded revolution,
which the Sanhedrin wouldn't tolerate since it threatened their
existence! He and they were on the same side, Caiphas continued, with only minor differences separating them, and they
subject to compromise.

I swear they said nothing at the time about killing him,
though I considered that a distinct possibility—and my hostility
to Jesus being so great I didn't care! I had been too often and
bitterly disappointed to sympathize with him. Besides, he had
a sixth sense of danger and had shown remarkable self-preservation skills when opposition grew lethal. Judging from past
events, he would find a way to defend himself—maybe by
pulling one of his vanishing acts. He *wouldn't* let himself be
killed, I was sure; he had too much ego for that; he thought too
highly of his role for that; he intended to see the end of Israel
and the temple! Indeed, how could anyone be a real threat to
teacher when he had been consistently invincible?

What an insightful man I was, they stressed, as our discussion continued, to see the issues so clearly and to
courageously resolve them by forcing a confrontation with
Jesus of Nazareth. My name would fondly be remembered in
Israel, they affirmed, as the man who stood in the breach
between powerful, sometimes antagonistic forces, to effect a
reconciliation from which all Israel would benefit. Men with
my capabilities would always be needed to supervise temple
vendors.

For three years I hadn't been shown a scintilla of the appreciation I received in those few minutes! I felt hope for the first

time in more than a year—and found myself at peace for the first time in nearly two. I had at last arranged the encounter that would save both Jesus and the leadership! And *I* would be remembered as the facilitator! Here were men with whom I had a perfect understanding!

Of course, it would be necessary to keep the agreement private, they murmured. Only members trusted to keep the confidence would be involved—which would exclude Joseph and Nicodemus, they noted.

Ignoring the threat latent in that condition, I merely asked them to take an oath on our agreement. They quickly complied, even swearing by the city and temple! Then, to show their good faith, and a token of their future generosity to me, they weighed out the silver coins. Never in all my discipleship days had I felt such weight in the money bag! What security it gave me, after all those months of financial penury. Of course, to eliminate suspicions from rabbi and the disciples, I had to secrete the funds in my personal money belt, where I kept a reserve for personal emergencies. On occasion I even put a little from the common purse there, as a reward for my responsibility and worry.

I took the money without guilt! I had gone without financial security for three years, worrying while rabbi spent! Why shouldn't I be rewarded? Rabbi would now hate me, and every disciple would want to kill me! I needed a reserve from which I could return to Kerioth and begin the import-export business my temple contacts made possible.

Concluding the meeting, Annas confided that they had already planned to isolate the Galilean after the feast, then hail him before the entire Sanhedrin. My arrival was possibly fortuitous to a change in plans. Since he could secretly leave the city after Passover and, with people scattering everywhere, lose himself in the crowds returning to Galilee, could I arrange his seizure in an isolated area *during* the feast? With the people at home, and the streets empty, the arrest could then be quietly effected. I quickly agreed, with the stipulation that I could guarantee it only for a short period, after which I would lose control of circumstances.

They assented. I had only to let them know rabbi's location and they would dispatch temple soldiers for him. Hardly anyone would know and no one would connect me with the event. When I remarked that I wouldn't know the meeting place for several days, they promised to be available at Caiphas' till I brought information.

I came to Olivet just before sunset with other late-arriving disciples, rabbi awaiting our return. I caught his glance. Did I see recognition I hadn't previously noticed? Did he give me an accusatory look? Did he *know*? Was anything ever a mystery to him? Would he inform the others? Would I suddenly feel a sharp blade slicing through me tonight? Together we ascended the summit, then quickly traveled the mile or so to the village, the distance it had taken so long to complete earlier in the day. Everyone's subdued mood, including rabbi's, deepened the enigma and intensified the malaise in my mind.

...AND TRIPPED

Rabbi foiled me! Arrangements hadn't yet been made for the Passover meal. He had so many friends with big houses, who welcomed him whenever he appeared, he seemed in no hurry to secure a host. Not wanting to arouse his suspicion, I asked nothing.

My anxiety flared as we climbed from the valley to the city. *How am I going to let the Sanhedrin know if I don't know myself? When will rabbi decide? As soon as he does I can get away and, with throngs everywhere, easily lose myself and make contact.*

Finally, late morning, the others asked—rabbi seemed absorbed in his thoughts—WHERE do we eat the Passover?

My hopes soared!

Then fell!

He gave Peter and John mysterious directions: go into a packed Jerusalem, find a *man* carrying a water pitcher and follow him to the house he served. There they would find the room.

Panic seized me: *he must suspect me. How have I been discovered? I've hidden my true feelings from everyone! But can anyone hide from rabbi? What else could account for this subterfuge? He wants to keep me from implementing my plan to save Israel! Rabbi's clever, I have to give him that; how many men will be carrying water jars?*

The arrest can't occur during the meal, I ruefully concluded, as Peter and John requested money from me, then left. *His arrest will now likely excite the very turbulence the authorities want to avoid! But I can't stop now! I'll have to find a way!*

Cursing my rotten luck, I secreted my feelings—continuing to wonder why he took that suspicious approach to getting a room. Always before, we made arrangements days before the feast. Now, in secret, rabbi plotted. It *had* to be against me!

Obviously he would go only to trusted friends. But who knew, it was likely someone so enamored of him that the mere opportunity would be welcomed, no matter the inconvenience.

He had that effect on people! It's possible he had ordered one of the disciples to make the arrangements earlier. But this had every indication of spontaneity, where his famous trust in God could be rewarded.

I knew I was right as we climbed through the Upper City. We passed several mansions where rabbi would have been generously hosted before arriving at a commodious house belonging to Mary, who had a young son Mark. Yes, I could have envisioned him coming *here*!

It's proximity to Caiphas' mansion commended it to me. But as we ascended the stairs, my mind raced: *how will I get away? Once inside the Upper Room, rabbi will never let me leave! He's outwitted me!*

Furious with his deceit, I followed the others, thinking of *bolting* while I had the chance, but afraid of arousing their suspicions and rabbi's fears—and he would simply go elsewhere. I thought about finding someone to run the news to Caiphas, but hadn't the time. In a depressed rage I followed into a large, well-furnished room, with couches and the ubiquitous u-shaped table, from which servants would bring, serve and remove dishes; lamps swaying in the gentle breeze, flickering against the dusk soon turning dark. Assorted chairs and tables scattered around the room, each a matched set, fresh flowers in vases adding color. Drapes covered the windows, but were drawn back, shutters open. Elements of the Passover Meal filled the table, the smell of roast lamb appealing, enchanting, distracting.

Everyone gathered ahead of me, the servants ready to wash our feet, especially important on a holy night when nothing unclean could impair the festivities.

And, in the instant I took in all the sights, I received the shock of my life. Looking beyond the rest rabbi gazed at me, then said, "Judas, you will be my guest tonight."

My eyes popped; my mouth dropped.

"Me, rabbi," I asked, hands pointed at my shoulders, all the while shouting mentally, *why me? Why now? You've always invited one of your Galileans. Why choose me when I want to stay as far as possible from you and get out of here as soon as possible? Do you know? Will you reveal my plans? Put me in the middle of everyone, closest to you, where I can't defend myself? How beguiling you are, hanging me by my thumbs, broiling me like sheep on a spit!*

Despite the blizzard of thoughts, charges, hatreds and questions blinding my mind, I merely gulped, "Thank you, rabbi, I'm most honored." With that subservient bootlicking, my shoulders fell and I walked behind the teacher to where he sat on his couch and beckoned me to mine. Dumbfounded, I sat. The servants in the room said nothing. The disciples stood in a group seething, their eyes flashing at rabbi and darting at me.

My question wasn't a tithe of their disconcertion. *"Why Judas?,* they wondered. *What's he done to receive this honor? Isn't he already Treasurer, the only real power-post among us? What else can he have next but the lay leadership? Is this rabbi's introduction to it?*

I knew the ingrates...the first time in three years rabbi acknowledged me, and they resented it. Since it interfered with my plans, I resented it even more!

Dumb with both disbelief and delight, I said nothing as rabbi motioned each man to his couch, John after me, then Peter and so on until we all sat.

In a way rabbi disarmed me. *Oh rabbi,* I thought as I sat there, *if only you had done this before! Why wait till now, when it's too late and I no longer trust you? This can't compensate for all the times you duped me. And now you think to reconcile me with this honor—now...after you have driven me away?*

If only you had been so gracious at first, when I trusted and loved you completely. If along the way, as I struggled with doubt, wanting to believe, you had drawn me aside and asked what was troubling me, I would have poured out my heart to you. You couldn't have been unaware, rabbi...not you with your blazing eyes cutting through me like scythes. If you had only asked my opinions, I would have gladly shared them; any patriot would. You could have trusted me; I want only what's best for my people.

Why did you wait so long—too long! Of all the grief you've caused me, this is the worst of all; when I no longer believe, you make me guest of honor! Let this be a lesson to you; honors coming too late are insults, not tributes! And how brazen to use this most sacred of meals to gain the advantage of my will!

*Now, suspicious of what I plan, you want me to change, thinking this triviality will compensate for your previous slights. Now **you're** begging, using a favor to seduce me. It won't work, rabbi; I'm not bargaining. Time was I would, but not now. The leaders are the only ones who can convince you now!*

I can't say how many similar reproaches blitzed my mind in those few minutes, everyone negative, hateful, accusatory!

How I could notice anything poignant, while infused with the rage I felt, I can't say, but I sensed his need of our companionship. If I hadn't already been hardened against him, it would have moved me to pity. He craved our fellowship as the starved crave food! Why this time, more than the other two Passovers I'd shared with him? Did he presciently see the future as something new and, for him, sinister?

Too busy bickering among themselves, the other disciple couldn't detect his emotions. As he sat and listened, they hissed words around the circle. Obviously, what had begun as a critique of me had turned into mutual verbal warfare. Jealous of me tonight, they were equally jealous of each other all day, every other day! It gave me savage satisfaction to see the myth of their disinterestedness in position exploded. It should have proved their low quality—the very men he had recruited, only to find them caustic of anyone else's success, particularly mine. For an instant, in golden silence, I heard the bickering as proof of how radically wrong rabbi had been in choosing the Galileans while ignoring Judean patriots!

I don't recall how long he and I sat silently while the men quarreled, threw hard looks and harsh words. Only when teacher loudly cleared his throat did he get their attention and silence their verbal jousting.

Then it happened, the hammer blow that split the diamond, rabbi's wordless activity that snapped my last reserves of tolerance and drove me to depart and—whatever the cost, however difficult, however much he tried to restrain me, if I had to fight my way out of there to meet the authorities—to deliver him up!

He said nothing...just took off his outer garment and wrapped a towel around his waist. He went to a stand, picked up a basin and walked over to me.

All eyes, wide and glistening, flickered in the lamps, astounded!

"Judas, I'll wash your feet now."

I sat transfixed, uncomprehending, scandalized. The servility enraged me. A provocation against position and authority! Had he no pride in himself? A man who claimed to be Messiah and God's Son acting like a common servant performing humiliating tasks?

The ferment of all the past months had finally brewed this absurdity? I had to act! I knew I would; now I knew I must! By being faithless to himself rabbi stacked the last in a heaping pile of evidence that proved he could never be worthy of me. I suddenly, violently and passionately loathed and wanted to harm him! Flashing hate for the man I had once considered the Son of God surged through me. I would never follow a man who couldn't separate the rational from the ridiculous.

Nevertheless, with contradictions battling, I calmly and supinely shuffled my feet to the floor. With the others I sat speechless while rabbi wet and toweled them. When finished, he looked at me with the strangest and deepest compassion I had ever seen from him—and I had often seen his compassion! I dropped my eyes while he passed to the others.

When finished, he resumed his place and asked if we knew what he had done. Of course we *knew*; we didn't know *why*! We dumbly nodded at the act, while animals in understanding. *He shouldn't have done this, he couldn't have done this,* we all shouted to ourselves, despite seeing it with our own eyes! *Not this man, who always had everyone supplicating his largesse! Who stood at bedside and raised the dead; who stood at bier-side and raised the dead; who stood at tomb-side and raised the dead, effortlessly, powerfully! Now this servility? Jesus obviously had no idea how greatness should behave!*

And when he spoke of being master and lord, I hardened my resolve: *never, rabbi! Though I once believed that, I do not now or ever again will! After all your talk of glory and power and being the basis of salvation or condemnation for all humanity, you have revealed yourself as a hopelessly idealistic FOOL!*

It shamed me into being ashamed I had ever trusted Jesus of Nazareth! What did I care that I heard a reference to a Psalm about someone lifting up a heel against him. *Exactly what someone should do,* I stormed to myself,...*kick some sense into your head!*

While I hadn't that power, I knew the men who did! And as I began to look for some reason to be excused—I don't feel well, rabbi...I forgot to offer alms today...I see we don't have enough bitter herbs for the meal—he gave me the perfect exit.

He suddenly sat up, and everyone stopped eating to watch. Obviously wanting to say something, but struggling with the words, he quietly and emotionally declared, "One of you will betray me."

The words struck like stone pillars falling from the sky. I was known! I couldn't keep secrets from rabbi! And, now, I was at his right hand, surrounded by the others, with no place out! I wanted to rid myself of bones and sinews, slide off the couch and slink away. I had been afraid, and my fears had come true. Like Haman before Queen Esther I was discovered, and now fearfully awaited rabbi's finger sticking in my face and his shouted anger, "This is the man!"

I grimaced inwardly and braced myself, my breaths became harder and quicker, sweat popped from my forehead and I tried to keep my eyes from darting everywhere, man to man, around the room, to the doors.

Then, unbelievably and providentially, teacher said nothing more. No one but I understood the meaning! Not a man there, myself included, but would admit to having betrayed him accidentally, by reason of their humanity, with their little faith, less wisdom, colossal ambition and unspoken criticism. Hadn't even Simon been called Satan months before? Did he also shrink before teacher's prediction?

Interestingly, every disciple in the room, me included to cover myself, stared first at each other and then, something I never expected from those petty men, asked pitifully, sorrowfully, aghast, "Is it I?"

Not given my perspective, they considered betrayal by one of us incomprehensible! *One of us?* We who had been so familiar with him, had eaten with him, lived with him, seen him every day, loved him so. *One of us?* No one would have been surprised if it had been someone in the larger group, or from a spy sent to watch his movements. But one of the Twelve? It couldn't be. How could *anyone* sink so low, least of all one of his own men?

Everyone sat and *stared* at each other, eyes questioning, eyebrows furrowing and pinching together, clamoring mentally, *maybe involuntarily, Master, but never intentionally would any of us betray you!, Never! Not a one of us but intends to be your faithful servant!*

How fortunate for me. Their increased guilt decreased mine, and I relaxed. Even more so when rabbi simply said, "It is one of the Twelve," limiting the source of the accusation, but leaving no doubt that he meant exactly what he had said—*one of us!*

Again, to my astonishment, he said nothing more. To my left I noticed Peter lean back against John and whisper something, then John lean back against the again-recumbent rabbi, and whisper something. Rabbi's whispered response revealed that it was one who dipped in the dish with him—which all Twelve had and would do again as he, the host, offered it to us.

One of us dipping, rabbi? I questioned. *Then you're protecting, not exposing me? Do you want to be arrested, questioned and forced to compromise with the leaders? Are you now looking for a way out of the dilemma your recalcitrance has created? Will you use me to achieve what you personally can't, figuring you can blame me for the act, though it's merely your way of escaping responsibility? Do I have permission to betray you? Are you using me even now to accomplish your will? I would rather you scold or harangue or denounce me—anything but protect me, since I don't want your protection and I don't want to do your will!*

Then he said the fatal words: "Woe to the man who betrays me." Instantly alert, I silently savaged him. *Woe to that man, rabbi? For saving the whole nation? Woe to me, when it's you who guaranteed the temple's destruction and Jerusalem's capture and Israel's banishment as slaves and wanderers? Woe to me?*

Woe to you, rabbi! You deceived people into thinking you would help them, but won't! You promised to free us from Rome, but haven't! Woe to you, erring rabbi, faithless to our fathers' traditions by insistence on obedience to you! I have

Israel on my side and the leadership as my patrons! What are
you compared to the whole nation? Why should patriots sit
idly by as you bring us to ruin? In a way, I guess, woe to me,
for I believed in another imposter-Messiah, who now wants to
be considered unsullied while tarring me with the blackest ep-
ithets.

This ferocious anger flared within me as he first accused,
then uttered his malediction. By an act of supreme self-control
I hid the rage and awaited his wrath.

He got off his couch and brought the bowl to me. I looked
just above his eyes as he offered it. "Is it I, rabbi," I whispered,
trying for steadiness in a room silent as death. I thought I
would choke on the words since I knew the next moment
would be my last.

He merely whispered—"You have said it." I helplessly
gazed into his eyes, and I couldn't believe the LOVE I
saw...love I couldn't deny—love I had seen in him on many occasions   when   people   came   seeking   him...love
gushing...cascading! It couldn't be, not love now, in this hour
of denial! I wanted to shout that he give up the charade, to
look me in the eye man to man and tell me he despised me as
much as I had grown to despise him, that he was as sorry he
had chosen me as a disciple as I was in being one. *Don't look*
at me that way, rabbi, I wanted to protest. *Mistreat me, abuse*
me, backhand me! For no one can be so favorable towards a
person who hates you so thoroughly, who can so easily resist
your kindness.

Instead I said nothing more, but wondered if the disciples
had heard us. Since they did nothing, I wondered if my
question might have been so quiet they didn't hear; or maybe
they felt such shock that words meant nothing; or did they
think rabbi was going to approach each one and hold a private
conversation before publicly identifying the culprit; or maybe
they were sincere about themselves personally being the betrayer, knowing how many times they had failed him; or could
they have merely equated *failing* with *betrayal,* despite rabbi's
malediction on a *betrayer*?

I had no clue; I knew only that the disciples remained inert,
and I sighed with relief when teacher went next to John,
bending close, John whispering, rabbi replying.

Within seconds, knowing that rabbi had, for whatever reason, chosen not to expose me, I had the strongest possible urge to GET OUT OF THERE IMMEDIATELY before he changed his mind. *Go and complete your task,* resolution clamored; *stand in the breach and save Israel from this man's errors and you can save him for Israel's future. The authorities want only to reach accord with him, and you'll be hailed as a hero! Up and out, man, now!*

Unbidden, unheralded, unspoken it all came to me—and I heard and obeyed!   As rabbi passed from John to Simon I slipped from my couch, put on my sandals, rabbi paying no attention, and walked around the couches towards the door, my spine tingling lest he might yet shout, "There's the man...seize him!"—knowing that at least two knives would reach my back before I reached the door.

Yet, in those interminable seconds, I swore I'd rather die on the spot trying to save rabbi and Israel from destruction than to live and see the nation perish before my eyes.

I closed the door behind me and felt the chilly wind, and only then did I realize how profusely I had perspired from the stress in that upper room. I rushed down the steps two at a time—and no one followed. I figured they thought rabbi had given me instructions to buy something lacking for the meal, or to give something to the poor.

"Free at last," I shouted aloud, once in the empty street. "Free at last, and now knowing *where* to secure rabbi's arrest!"

In minutes I arrived at the High Priest's house, carrying with me the emancipation of my people—and, if rabbi would only be reasonable, his own best interests. In that carefree mood I stopped at the gate to Caiphas' mansion. A guard holding a blazing torch peremptorily dismissed me, saying I would get no handouts there, that I was to go elsewhere, that the High Priest was hosting the Passover with the most important men of the nation.

I coldly told him I had news the High Priest must hear. "What news?.," he grumped more acidly. Unwilling to bear his temerity, I shouted at him, "Tell him Judas Iscariot is here, and do it now if you value your life!"

Shaken by my equally peremptory outburst, he handed the torch to another guard, turned and reluctantly ascended the steps to the magnificent palace that housed Israel's hopes.

Just think, I boasted to myself, *in a few minutes I'll be the most important man those important men have ever seen—I, Judas Iscariot, unknown Judean, unappreciated disciple of a Galilean rabbi—for I have information where they can find the man who has so tormented them and disappointed me!* When the guard returned *running*, I knew I'd succeeded!

ARREST AND TRIAL

Ananias sent messengers and forewarned-security congregated in the courtyard. By the first hour of the second watch, the officer felt he had sufficient force to discharge his responsibility, despite my protests of overkill: why recruit a couple hundred armed men to arrest one peace-loving man? The captain calmed me: after all, rabbi did have eleven men with him who could be counted on to fight; and didn't I say they were armed with at least two swords?

With enough lanterns and torches to light the way, we exited the Golden Gate and began a tension filled trip to Olivet. It occurred to me that almost five days before rabbi had been mobbed by thousands in this very gate—hadn't seized the moment, and now would pay for his indecision.

To secure surprise, the captain ordered silence and all lights extinguished until we were there, ready for action. If rabbi saw the necklace of light winding down the hill to the valley, he would be alerted and have ample time to flee. Swiftly as the terrain allowed, sometimes two or three abreast, sometimes several more, we marched down the switchbacks leading to the Kidron. Malchus, as special representative of the High Priest, accompanied us, reminding the captain that his highness wanted the Galilean arrested no later than the end of the second watch and in their clutches immediately after. For good or ill, events had slipped from my into the priests' hands, and I could only trust them to keep faith with me.

Those accustomed to night marches found secure footing in the bright moon and unclouded sky; the rest of us stumbled along. Ghostly shapes rose before us as we approached, to be identified as palms, boulders and terraces as we drew abreast. In the valley, picking our way, we saw the hills beyond. Again ordered to silence, we ascended, shuffling sandals scooping dirt into low clouds.

All the while I wondered at the reception rabbi would give the troops. He had never been timorous when dealing with the leaders, but that was in the presence of supporters, or neutral listeners. In them he always found refuge; their very numbers kept him safe. How would he react to a hostile crowd? Perhaps the High Priest had planned more wisely than I. As unpredictable as rabbi had become, it was better safe with too many than in peril with too few troops.

And what response would *I* get from him, especially to the identifying kiss I had to give? I made my plans: as soon as I marked him, I'd melt into the crowd, letting others arrest him.

Almost exploding with anxiety, I finally saw above me the olive grove I knew housed the olive press. Here my acquaintance became essential. I had to distinguish rabbi's small group and campfire from dozens of others girdling the mountain. Then, having isolated them from the rest, I had to particularly identify rabbi. In the dark, even with lighted torches, faces could easily be disguised, especially if one intended to hide.

The Sanhedrin feared that if they had to *search* for Jesus, the distraction would give him time to flee. They insisted that I accompany the troops and lead them directly to their prey.

After surveying the area, and dismissing unfamiliar voices and faces, I stopped and raised a hand. The captain repeated my gesture, halting the column. I pointed to an enclosure about thirty yards uphill, guarded by a hedge and gate. "There," I whispered.

"Be absolutely sure," he whispered back. "I can't return empty-handed. Take time to verify."

I spoke softly: "Beyond the gate you'll find a press, beyond that a second gate leading to the owner's private garden. He's rabbi's follower, and we've often stayed there. He'll be there, no doubt."

"Probably hiding," he chuckled grimly, then whispered orders for his men to surround the entire grove. They would be given half an hourglass to get into position. On hearing the shout, "The sword of the Lord," each would light his torch or lantern and seal the area to prevent escape until the suspect was identified and secured.

The minutes dragged by before the officer and Malchus suddenly shouted the great shout. A circle of fire from lighted torches and lanterns enveloped the garden and men *charged*, breaking down the gate and, from all directions poured through, sweeping up a terrified riff-raff like fish in a net.

From all directions came the irresistible force of light and soldiers, shouting, thumping and pounding clubs against the trees. People screamed imprecations as they roused from sleep or from pleasant campfire reveries. In those chaotic, thrilling seconds torches turned the whole garden into an eerie twi-light as hundreds milled inside the impenetrable soldier-cordon.

I kept searching for rabbi among all the faces bobbing momentarily into sight. Then, THERE he stood, silently and solemnly, unafraid and unmoved by the terror of people fleeing towards and past him, vainly seeking shelter from their fears. Simon, James and John were with him—*some things don't change*, I mentally noted—and soon other disciples leaked through the melee and hugged him in despair, the light magnifying the terror in their eyes. The jostling crowd tried to flee but, like startled minnows, only dashed back and forth, still surrounded by menacing temple guards. Everything remained tumultuous until the captain shouted in exasperation, "Stop this screaming. You're in no danger from us. We want only one man and his disciples. The rest of you can go."

Calm came in stages; when quiet returned, rabbi stepped from the disciples and walked towards me. He stopped a few feet away, his disciples following. He looked at me with a searching stare, which I confess I couldn't return. Then, to security, "Whom do you seek?"

"Jesus of Nazareth."

"I AM he."

What happened next I can't say, except an invisible but irresistible force hit us and we all fell around rabbi like flower petals, those closest to him collapsing against those behind until, around the entire circle, people lay in heaps, clamped to the ground by an unwalled prison.

When it happened, the innocents gathered in the net screamed and scampered over the prone bodies, leaving only rabbi and the eleven.

Like statues mesmerized by the voiceless power binding us, we lay there while he surveyed the scene. After what seemed an eternity, he quietly called us erect. How strange: in an unwalled prison we lay until freed by the one we came to arrest! Whatever held us instantly vanished and we rose to our feet, the surging blood stinging our limbs.

Again, "Whom do you seek?"

"Jesus of Nazareth."

But this time nothing—was it a portent? Had teacher issued a warning that he couldn't be *taken* by us, but would willingly *give* himself to us?

The officer turned to me, "*Is* this the man?"

"Yes," I replied and stepped forward.

The disciples couldn't believe their eyes. In all the commotion my presence hadn't registered with them. Now, in the leaping light their shocked faces glared at me with unspoken, shuddering rage—*Judas, you monster; are you mad? You fool!*—but what did I care?

As I stepped forward, the disciples instinctively moved away. I held out my arms, touched rabbi's shoulders, brushed my beard against his, turned to the left and lightly touched his cheek with my lips. "Rabbi," I whispered.

He stood stoically. Then, as I lingered momentarily, wanting to explain why I'd done it, why it was for his own good, that he'd thank me when it was all over, he pulled inches away and caught my eyes head-on in a glistening fixation; then, with a resigned accusation asked, "Judas, are you betraying the Son of Man with a kiss?" I hastily muttered that the priests demanded positive identification, then slipped away, backing off as the troops surged.

Rabbi shouted a command and, strangely, everyone stopped. "I said I'm the one you seek," his voice powerful and intimidating. "That being true, let these men go."

A thoughtful instant followed, then, from the captain, "As you say. Turn and be manacled." Before he finished the command, Malchus, who hated him merely by association, swore at rabbi and reached to seize him. As instantly Peter impulsively stepped in front, unsheathed his sword and struck. Flashing in the light, its glint caught Malchus' eye seconds before it slashed and caught his ear, slicing it cleanly away.

A deranged bellow leaped from Malchus as blood oozed, spurted and ran down inside his garments. "Rabbi, rabbi, he cut me," he roared. "Please rabbi, help me! My ear is gone, I'm bleeding to death."

I suddenly feared for teacher's life. The guards couldn't let him escape or would pay with their own lives! Would they think it necessary to slay him to prevent further bloodshed?

Jesus again assumed control. Seizing Peter's left arm, he commanded, "Put that sword away!" Then, preventing further provocation, and as if still tending to business as usual, he quietly touched Malchus' ear. When he pulled back, a murmur swept over the soldiers and disciples—not only had the blood dried and vanished but a new ear had appeared!

And Malchus, so swift to arrest the man he had hated, and now obligated to him for healing, in a state of shock, eyes full moons, stammered repeatedly through his tears—"Thank you, rabbi, thank you, thank you."

When the guards stepped forward to seize Jesus, the disciples fled. Their teacher wouldn't let them help him, wouldn't let them keep him from arrest, wouldn't let them defend him with their own lives—and in the hysteria of that awareness bolted like quail.

I watched rabbi weakly submit to arrest. As they bound him, he lectured them about this being their hour, as if protesting words equaled swords and clubs!

I had conflicting thoughts! I was wrong; he wouldn't defend himself from arrest, as I hoped, but surrendered himself like a lamb! Who could have anticipated it? Whenever confronting the leadership he proved masterful. Now, by night—had the night arrest shaken him, robbed him of his initiative, his energy, his confidence?—he *let* himself be led away. Or...did he want a meeting with the leaders? What an enigma!

For the first time in a year, I felt a twinge of conscience. What had I done? Seeing rabbi react so solicitously towards Malchus disturbed as it moved me. How could I betray a person who would take time in that maelstrom to perform a miracle—for a sworn enemy! Whatever he did, rabbi became increasingly mysterious to me.

Then I lectured myself for becoming sentimental, *remember, Israel needs a strong, not a gentle Messiah; a warrior who wields the sword, not a healer of severed ears!*

But the guilt grew—and finally cannibalized me!

Surrounded by guards, rabbi willingly conceded as they first pushed, then shoved him around, securing him between two of their strongest men for the trip back.

I fell through the advancing column, torches and lanterns passing me. *My part is finished. Nothing now but to follow and see what happens.* "Please, God, help rabbi co-operate with the authorities!", I whispered.

Through a lax security guard—a *girl* on duty in this most important building!—we entered the gate of the High Priest. Knowing that some of the disciples might regain their courage and follow, I found a place safe from their vengeance.

Security took teacher to Annas' compound, acknowledging his role as power broker between Pilate and the leadership. I knew it was the first of three trials, but why the rush? It wasn't legal to meet before daylight, and the leaders had promised a private discussion with rabbi—which could certainly wait till daylight. I figured they would welcome him as a lost brother, wine and dine him, then enter into serious negotiations, knowing how many followers he had all over Judea, Perea and Galilee.

Yet here we were, standing in the courtyard waiting while inside the leaders *couldn't* wait to convene proceedings. Had they forgotten their pledge? Had they devised another agenda from the first and used me to achieve it? Were there no honest men in Israel?

Not allowed inside, many still stood close enough to hear as conversations and words tumbled from the chambers mouth to mouth until they rolled to the last rows of spectators. I began to edge closer to the action, anxious to see if my goals had been achieved. Maybe this preliminary hearing was necessary to let rabbi know what would be discussed when the full Sanhedrin later met.

The news filtering out unsettled me, however, because it already portended open conflict between him and the leaders, along with rumors of him being physically struck by an officer for being disrespectful of the High Priest.

This wasn't what I planned!

Not long afterwards—after the first hour of the third watch—Annas dismissed the proceedings to the hall of justice at Caiphas' with the entire Sanhedrin in attendance. Still manacled and surrounded by guards, rabbi trudged by close enough for me to touch him.

Unease lashed me! The unusual haste again belied their pledge! I didn't know if this had been a good idea, after all. Rabbi had his faults, as I had continually noted, but no one like him had ever been seen in Israel!

Had he been too unyielding in their presence, maintaining his flinty independence? Had the leadership simply taken advantage of me to seize him under duplicitous pretenses? Did both sides share the blame? A nagging sense of impropriety mounted as I conjectured the unthinkable: my goals might not be reached.

I followed the crowd to Caiphas' quarters and witnessed the death of my dreams. Alerted by those disrupted in the garden, throngs from all over the city had gathered in the courtyard. Determined to be an eyewitness, I patiently edged to the front of the line closest to the hall, where I could see and hear. I silently prayed that, with my contribution to Israel's history over, seminal discussions would occur inside the fabled hall that would eventually re-establish our hegemony over the land.

I saw between the Sanhedrin and crowd a hedge of sphinx-like soldiers at attention, feet apart, spears at sides, backs to the participants. I saw the semi-circle of judges, faces contorted with hate, verbally abusing rabbi, who stood before them, silent and solemn. And, as each moment passed, despair grew bleaker and darker and further unhinged me.

Palpable menace stormed my hopes.

Still, at the beginning of the third hour of the third watch, rabbi seemed rested and radiant, for all the exhaustion he must have felt, being now over twenty hours since he slept. He stood manacled but unbowed, listening, perhaps waiting his chance to speak and convince the leaders, as he had so many others. If he would ever make his point, impress people and convince Israel, he had to do it now...in public assembly with the leaders. By having them together, he faced his golden moment. "Please God, let him seize it, and all will be well," I called aloud. "Assert yourself now, rabbi," I called even louder, to no one in particular. "Bargain, beg or surrender, anything to stay alive and keep teaching!"

The High Priest's clerk repeatedly gavelled a call to order and the crackling cacophony gradually diminished, then disappeared—the silence disturbed only by voices floating in from the courtyard below.

To my astonishment, looking around I saw Simon Peter standing not ten yards away. My heart accelerated, then re-

turned to normal as I assured myself he could do me no harm—
and, with his eyes fixed on rabbi, didn't even see me! As the
High Priest began, I saw rabbi lift his head, turn from the semi
circle and sweep a gaze over the audience, as if seeing who was
there. I'm sure he looked straight at me, but how could he see
me amongst the many?

Caiphas stated their brief—to my astonishment, lethal and
menacing—not the approach I had conceived and had been told
by the leaders to expect. Not, "we've brought Jesus of
Nazareth here to openly discuss differences and to reach
common ground," but, "we had him arrested as a false prophet
deluding the people and we intend to present irrefutable evidence that convicts him."

Booing and hissing rippled through the crowd; but I
KNEW: Caiphas' "convicts him" left no doubt about his goals,
especially as he asked, "Is there anyone here who has evidence
of this man's false teaching?"

I argued angrily, vocally. "They should know if he taught
falsely," I said to no one in particular. "They're in charge of
our religion."

Deafening silence followed, embarrassing Caiphas and
causing restless shifting by men on the benches.

"Come now," Caiphas shouted to the packed throng, "this
man can't harm you for telling the truth. We have him in our
power and intend to prosecute him for his misdeeds. You're
under our protection, so don't be afraid. Now, then, who will
be the first to testify against him?"

Prosecute him, I heard, but not much else, for the word reinforced "convicts him!" And all of them glared with
inconsistency from what I had expected. They had already
decided rabbi's guilt and sought only hostile witnesses. This is
what we expected from Romans, not from our own leaders.
"Give rabbi a break!", I heard myself clamoring aloud, "a
chance to admit he's been too zealous for reform, to agree he
sees the issue more clearly now that he understands how deeply
he has offended and alienated you!"

A lusty certainty overcame me, however: he wouldn't have
that chance.

After what seemed forever, voices responded to Caiphas'
second appeal. "I heard him say Moses didn't give us the right
to divorce our wives." Another, "he consistently healed on the

Sabbath day." Another, "he regards Gentiles as our equals, even saying they will be in the kingdom and we banished from it." Each charge met with murmuring approval of a few but with scorn from many in the crowd as they registered opposition to the charges point by point: "He stressed God's intention of marriage." "Why shouldn't the Sabbath be a day of deliverance instead of the burden it's become?" "Who's to say Gentiles can't know God?"

One man remembered rabbi's intention to destroy the temple and in three days build another. I winced as I heard it—one of those hasty, provocative remarks enemies could turn into malicious slander. And here it was, hanging out like dirty laundry. But even that was contradicted by a sharp thinker who replied that rabbi was always saying something hard to explain—and it probably being symbolic, why choose that instance as evidence?

On occasion, as someone in the crowd said something, the silent teacher turned, looked, listened, deliberated, totally-controlled! I was seeing him in a different light—an admirable man! It brought back sensations of my first impressions in the temple three years before. Had I *erred* by handing him over? Worse, had I **sinned?** Did the leaders intend to make a public spectacle of him, to humiliate him before all Israel so he would never again be able to influence people—to so shame him he wouldn't risk being in public, preaching in public, healing in public or anything in public that would encourage people to recall these moments? Maybe he would have to leave Israel and go to the Gentiles.

Sensing the futility of his witnesses, Caiphas finally stepped forward and personally challenged rabbi. "Are you saying nothing, with all these people accusing you? Here's your chance for rebuttal! You don't need anyone to defend you, you're so wise. You've always had an answer for our questions and have often posed unanswerable questions for us, now speak up! What's your response to these charges?" The men in the semi-circle, growing commensurably agitated, began to lose control and shouted, "Yes, speak for yourself, Nazarene—what can you say in rebuttal?"

Nothing. Complete, suffocating silence from the rabbi as he stared ahead, not even deigning to recognize the voices attacking him.

Caiphas couldn't contain his rage. He leaped forward and raised his right hand, threatening to slap Jesus across the face. Only a gasp from the crowd startled him to awareness, and he regained his composure.

Realizing that he had to put Jesus under oath to get any answer, he asked the most basic question possible—one the Sanhedrin had been pressing him to answer clearly: "Are you the Christ?"

"Hear! Hear!" exploded all over the Sanhedrin as members stood and shook their fists at the Galilean, daring him to answer!

Rabbi straightened himself as erect as his manacled arms would allow and spoke quietly and powerfully, his word carrying deep into the crowd, including to me, "I AM, and you will see the Son of Man sitting at the right hand of the Mighty One and coming on the clouds of heaven." It stunned me. I couldn't believe it. He declares it now, of all times? When for three years he replied enigmatically to their requests? When it was becoming increasingly evident that, lacking real evidence from others, they would have to wring it out of his own mouth, now, at the worst possible time, when the very declaration would push the Sanhedrin beyond simple punishment to execution—rabbi **declared** himself God's Anointed!—boldly, his voice ringing like a trumpet—I AM, words guaranteed to destroy.

Oh, rabbi, I inwardly exclaimed, *if only you had done that months ago when deputations from the Sanhedrin asked. The matter would have been discussed and compromised and it would never have come to this. It's now too late, rabbi, and at the wrong time; forced from you under oath, not given of your own free will!*

The brown eyes in his ferocious face snapping contempt, Caiphas tore at his collar and, turning to the leaders, cried, "What do you say, since he's condemned himself?"

Flaming denunciation assented as men stood, nearly frothing at the mouth. Everyone talked at once, their fists doubled. In turn, they approached Jesus, walking ominously close, staring at him, some even spitting in his face—"Oh, no, he doesn't deserve that," I murmured, tears welling. "He's a good man. Don't spit in his face—let him go, he's harmless, he's only been carried to extremes by his zeal for God. Haven't other prophets? Didn't they all seem strange? Didn't John—and you didn't spit in his face! Challenge him, correct him, criticize him, make him accountable, but don't strip away his dignity by spitting in his face!"

Their violence re-ignited division in the crowd—some delighted, some ashamed, some coming to blows over the treatment we could all see, but none of us could believe or stop.

With difficulty Caiphas called the Sanhedrin to order and motioned to the guards, who raised their spears to attack position as the clerk shouted he would clear the hall if any further disturbances occurred. After order gradually returned, leaving a rumbling like distant thunder, Caiphas herded the Sanhedrin to their benches. Then, despite a supreme effort to restrain himself, he again raved, "You have heard the blasphemy. What do you think?"

They rose as one man and shouted almost in unison, "guilty as charged and worthy of death!"

For some unknown reason, rabbi turned from them, as if hearing something else, forced his eyes into the crowd—as anyone who had been with him knew only he could do—searching for someone, boring ruthlessly until he found him, then focused there! Out of the corner of my eye I saw someone shoving and demanding to have room made, that he had to get out of there—and when I turned to see, it was Simon Peter! Our eyes locked—his full of tears—then he turned and continued bullying his way toward the courtyard.

While this distraction occurred, other gasps and groans drew my attention to the front—and I saw members of the Sanhedrin leap from the benches, walk up to Jesus and, in brawling indignation, begin beating him about the head and shoulders, all the while spitting on him and mocking him. Someone tied a blindfold on rabbi, and, holding his chin, repeatedly slapped his face, chortling, "Who's hitting you? You're so wise. Tell me who's hitting you?

What had I done? I asked myself, quivering in despair! I thought rabbi had been unreasonable, but now I know it's the Sanhedrin! They don't want to talk to him; they want him out of the way...silenced...dead...today!

Rabbi would inevitably be killed, for he obviously wouldn't defend himself! If he had only kept silent, the crowd's influence might have gained his release. Like me, many in the crowd had become increasingly sympathetic towards him as the leaders wickedly abused him. But when such a claim was purely inflammatory, he declared himself the Christ! When it could have been very useful, he avoided it. When it destroyed him, he affirmed it! Why would I never understand this man? Why wouldn't he let himself be understood?

Still, no one deserved the abuse he received—no one, certainly not an innocent person like rabbi. How terribly wrong I had been! He had often angered me, confused me, irritated me, but now, I felt thoroughly ashamed of myself—and didn't know what to do!

REMORSE AND DEATH

I stood in the courtyard hiding my face but couldn't escape the disgrace unfolding before me. Rabbi would be taken to Pilate for crucifixion!

It was all over for rabbi. He had offered in defense only what convicted him; they had carefully allowed nothing in exoneration. And if he had raised only words against the Jews, he wouldn't raise swords against the Romans. He would certainly be crucified before the day passed. Nausea saturated me, followed by a fever that convulsed, than a sweat that soaked me. My equilibrium failed, and I nearly collapsed.

No future existed for me. Too ashamed to even think I had a role in this scandal, I was more ashamed to consider seeking forgiveness. I sat in a stupor, staring, traumatized, blinking uncomprehendingly, drunk with apathy I couldn't shake, mental blackouts threatening me, a coercive exhaustion crushing me!

Then, like a wild animal aroused from its wounding, horrors I couldn't control stirred me to maniacal frenzy and I ran screaming into the night, sobbing hysterically, dark streets mute witnesses to my orgy. "Wasn't this what you wanted," a voice within repeatedly taunted, only to hear my repeated hysterical reply, "No it isn't, not this, not *this*, not by far!"

In turn, I raged at rabbi, denouncing him for betraying me by refusing to defend himself. I cursed him for not being conciliatory with the leaders so they wouldn't have found his death necessary. I chastened him for not performing a last minute miracle to escape death. Then, shouting my defiance of *their* treachery, I roundly damned the leaders for callously manipulating my patriotism to their personal vendetta.

Suddenly the weight of silver around my waist screamed an accusation against my betrayal. With the rare lucidity that delirium often brings, I decided to disavow my act by returning the money, convinced that it would vindicate me, heal my wounds and erase the tormenting pain, perhaps even motivate the Sanhedrin to free him!

Towards the middle of the third watch I knocked at the gate of the now-empty courtyard. A servant asked my business,

then walked away, telling me to wait. He came back slowly.
"How different from the last time," I ruminated angrily, spiting
his insolence. Without speaking he led me into Caiaphas'
house.

Only a smattering of members lounged in the chamber,
none of them my former confederates. When I asked for the
high priest, they curtly replied that he couldn't be spared, but
had left them in charge and what did I need?

Bitterness towards them replaced my grief, and I raved,
"You've deceived me by condemning him—and him innocent
of your charges. That was your plan all along, wasn't it, to use
my idealism to eliminate him? You promised to keep him safe,
you monsters! To question and correct him, but to secure his
life!"

"I'm guilty, do you hear?" "Guilty!" I shrieked. I've
sinned by betraying innocent blood! Don't you understand?
What I did was despicable! I can't find a way to justify it, and
I can't take this shame!"

The pompous asses stood there, arms across their chests,
smirking, "What do we care about this tardy attack of conscience?" they replied scornfully. "Or about your personal
struggle over the guilt you *now* feel? We kept the bargain you
made. We would have paid any amount you demanded. Is it
our fault you valued the teacher as nothing more than a slave?
You have your money; take it and go. We have nothing further
to say."

"Well, I have something to say to you, you blind guides"—I
couldn't believe I so insolently berated the most powerful men
of the nation, in whom I once had absolute confidence—"You
hypocrites, rabbi was right in everything he said about you.
You exploit a person's patriotism, you lie and cheat to get your
way, you make promises and break them when it pleases you,
you whited walls, filled with dead men's bones, how dare you
promise you wanted only to discuss your differences with
rabbi, when all the while you intended to condemn and execute
him. You saw me merely as a pawn to get your way. You de-
generate charlatans!

"And here's what I think of your money"—I slammed it on
the stone floor in front of them, bursting the bag, and out the
coins rolled. They stood agape at my ferocity, but lost none of

their arrogance. I continued. "I now understood why rabbi refused to negotiate with you hypocrites! You're in office for personal gain, not national responsibility. How could I have been such a fool *to trust you*! Damned fools! Damned liars!"

Out of the hall I erupted, every sandal a grinding disavowal of the Sanhedrin. Gaining speed and momentum as I reached the gate, held open by the servant, I began running all-out, anxious to flee that house of iniquity, that den of thieves whose dishonesty would as surely bring destruction on Israel as rabbi's idealism!

Now I had no idea what to do. Every alternative collapsed into laughable implausibility. Should I go to rabbi and beg forgiveness? But how could I do that; how could I even get close, with him under Roman guard? And how would he respond if I did? Didn't he say that it was better for the man who betrayed him never to be born? What could that mean *but* that I've fatally compromised my place with him!

Should I seek the disciples and confess my wrong? But what a stupid thought! They would kill me on *approach*! Should I return to Caiaphas' and repair the damage my tantrum caused? But the very thought of seeing those frauds repulsed me!

So into the night I walked...everywhere...commiserating with myself... interrogating myself... accusing myself...exonerating myself, a shadow of the man I had been only hours before, of the man I had hoped to become, but could never again be. Up and down dark streets I paced, hugging walls to keep from being recognized, frequenting back streets to retain my privacy, hunched...witless...harried, noticing the unusual furor as people rushed by, the words "Jesus of Nazareth" heard everywhere.

Wherever I went, guilt, shame and oppression followed!

Now, in the cool morning, I find the odium so loathsome and exhausting that I see no reason to live. I can't believe the abortion of my plans. Rabbi is by now condemned by Pilate and will soon be on his way to crucifixion. And how strange that I would even think of teacher now, since I long ago mentally divorced him!

What's left? What can I do to show God I'm sorry? I can't reverse the mistake, regretful as I am. As I look forward, I *see* nothing; and seeing nothing, I fear! What can I do but...I can hardly say the word without revulsion, I feel so powerfully about living—but it's the only word that sounds right— *SUICIDE!* Since I could never again face anyone, not even my own family, what else matters? Since I'm all alone in the world, what else is left?

How could my life end so ingloriously when it had such promise? What cruel fate connected me to rabbi? Why couldn't he have left me in the crowds, watching and applauding? Why did he ever call me to permanent discipleship, so I could learn more than I wanted to know...so much that I grew disenchanted with him? Oh, I could have been completely happy had I known him only superficially! Why couldn't he have been satisfied with that? I *now* would! Far better to have kept my distance and remained appreciative than to have despised him in intimacy! Oh, God, I'm poorer than ever, worse than ever, more lost than ever! Despair brutalizes me. Apathy consumes me!

Yet, how could I justify self-murder, life's ultimate negative, the denial of all the positive teachings of old and of rabbi himself? But how could I not consider it, given all that's happened? I'm absolutely abandoned by everyone, including rabbi, including God, so what's left? It's too late to recover any of the infamy. Rabbi's arrested and on his way to execution, and I may as well be dead!

This is the result of three years of selfless devotion! Rubble everywhere, hopes dashed, shattered dreams mocking! At one time, hating him for not rising to my aspirations, I refused to fall to his. But I can no longer say it was his fault, or mine; or who had the greater fault, he or I. I once thought him guilty and I innocent. Now I don't know, can't say, and don't care! He certainly didn't fulfill my dreams, but neither did I meet his expectations.

Is this how God rewards faithful service?

People will accuse me of treason. But how can I be guilty of that when, in every circumstance, I've been true to my convictions? "How could he do it?" people will repeatedly ask. "How could one so honored by his rabbi turn so dishonorably against him?" I cannot unequivocally reply. At some point in life we surrender to either fear or to faith. Did I give unreasonable freedom to my skepticism so that I reaped this cata-strophe? Did I get so tired of trying to understand rabbi that I simply wanted out and would do anything to get out, even to risking a bad decision just to escape what had become intol-erable?

Yet, what did he leave me but gravel on which I grind my teeth? Even as I admit there's no one in Israel who even ap-proximates him, didn't his blinding will-power pose unknown perils for our people? Indeed, if he were not well–intentioned, he would be maniacal. Well-intentioned as he is, he's easily still the most dangerous man in our history!

However I rationalize, I cannot justify betraying the man who genuinely tried to be my friend; who offered me ac-ceptance I found with no one else; against whom I made the decision to sever myself!

Even now I see that face, HIS face that often I saw, but wished to never see again. That face...his eyes..how piercingly they look on me in this darkness as they looked upon me in the Upper Room. Away, away, eyes of Christ. It's too late. You loved me and I hated you in return. You cared for me, and I be-trayed!

Still they probe uninterruptedly, compassion flowing...but it cannot be. Not after my wickedness. Close to my face he comes, eye to eye, nose to nose, his gaze like lightning bolts tearing through. Will he raise his hand to strike me as I saw him slapped at Caiphas'?

Now he's on his knees before me, outer coat off, wash basin full, hand towel around his waist, stopping at my couch, bending to his knees and looking at me with unconditional love.

Suddenly, the love I despised last night as weakness I view as unmeasured strength!

But not for me, not for me, given my sin. No, no, turn from me, face of Jesus, turn away forever!

Suddenly he's gone, I'm still alone in the dark, sweat pours off my face and I huddle against the chill of a canyon damp with dew and alive with shrill insects' chirping.

Even as I grieve over my betrayal, I offer an explanation. He had the perfect opportunity when arrested to declare his messianic identity. And for an instant I hoped he would; with joy I fell to the ground in the garden before his majesty. *Had the time finally come*, I questioned? *Had my endeavor finally prompted his reprisal against arrest*?

But no, the fire that flashed in his words perished with their expression, and he *let* himself be led away. Not even Peter's striking Malchus stirred his patriotism. Surely the smell of blood would have prompted his demand for a crusade against the occupier of our holy land, making agreement with the leadership to achieve it! But, no; instead of an order for the authorities to unsheathe their swords came an order for Simon to sheathe his!

Then to let himself be arrested with only a tongue-lashing of his tormenters? When he could have incinerated the whole, each word a firestorm! In my wildest nightmares I couldn't image rabbi helpless before the temple officials, sacrificing himself to degrading indignity; not Jesus of Nazareth, with his power!

How can I believe anything *except* he got what he deserved? If you don't use the power you have to defend yourself, what kind of man are you, after all? When only expressing it guarantees your continued possession of it, if self-preservation can't motivate, how can you expect sympathy from anyone?

When posterity has exhausted its adoration in volumes about rabbi, perhaps someone will speak a kind word for me. If posterity only knew what it cost me to deny him, it would sympathize instead of damning me. Indeed, I feel more sorrow turning rabbi over than he could possibly feel being arrested; I'm enduring the greater punishment while he committed the greater wrong!

Many will shrug in dismay trying to explain my behavior. Let them condemn me who have never had unresolved doubts and questions about God! When one has seen his hopes as bitterly shattered as I by rabbi, why should I feel badly for shattering his? Who did the greater disservice?   And who committed the greater sin against Israel, he or I?

Others will wonder how I could overlook all of his miracles, claims and teachings to even *consider* alienation. If they had matured in the political atmosphere so prevalent among many groups in Israel, mine included, they might be more critical of rabbi's unwillingness to negotiate with the patriots, or at least to listen to our views before converting us to his.

Besides, if he really were Messiah, would he have failed to convince *so many* in Israel? The upper class? At least the thinkers and leaders? If no one else, at least everyone of the Twelve? Surely history will favor me with this empathy: that rabbi bears the responsibility for not convincing each man of the Twelve! He certainly owed us that!

At the time I felt perfectly comfortable turning teacher over. Why wouldn't I? I saw it as an opportunity to end the three year war between an increasingly hostile Sanhedrin and teacher's obstinate unwillingness to publicly declare himself!

Committed to rabbi at first, I saw the flash of gold in his every miracle and word. Then...was it a conscious reaction...? I don't know. Did I make it quickly or slowly...? I can't say, my perceptions began to change. Reason and emotion both objected. Points of friction developed, not lubricated by rabbi's desire to reach me or my sudden intention to stay beyond reach.

At first I lectured my doubts, alarmed at my boldness, uneasy about the very contemplation of suspecting a man whose persona had won me. As more and more occasions of doubt came, however, and I became equal parts admiration and apprehension, rabbi both attracting and repelling me, I felt less the need to lecture myself and more the right to critique him. Until the day came when I could unequivocally disregard, then mentally dismantle him. So that by the collapse of the Galilean campaign I had become irrevocably opposed to him as the man who first resurrected, then assassinated my dreams. Was he not just a man like myself? I began to say. Was his light that bright, after all? For all his promise of our sitting on twelve thrones, judging Israel, didn't our sitting on hard ground around blazing campfires after three years mock his words?

I found rabbi unwilling to harm his enemies while continuing to alienate his friends. He had to be controlled for, given his truculence towards the priests, they would eventually kill him. I merely expedited the confrontation. To be helpful in achieving *reconciliation* between the warring parties, I turned him over, I want posterity to understand! Indeed, to rescue them from a conflict neither wanted but seemed powerless to prevent, I knew he had to be contained. Let my name be under an eternal curse if that wasn't my goal! I never intended to harm rabbi! He misunderstood my motives, if he thinks otherwise. I never meant his arrest to eventuate in his death! Can't he understand that?

And didn't he give me permission to betray him, almost demanding I quickly do it—perhaps, I thought—so he could the sooner prove himself to me? Would I have ultimately done it without teacher's unspoken but clear command?

After all, he allowed me to leave the room unidentified by him and untouched by the others. Had he wanted to avoid arrest, he need only beg me to reconsider or, God forbid, mention my name and traitor in the same sentence. For then both swords in the room would have been put to immediate use! Even if posterity considers me unthinkably treacherous, didn't certain rabbis conclude that God himself created the evil impulse, after which he repented? If that's true, am I really accountable for a misdeed even God is sorry he made possible?

God, why have you cast me out, against my will?

RETROSPECT

As I think about it now in this oppressive place, I see my mistake. I became gradually disaffected, and many times decided to leave because of it, only to change my mind and decide to stay knowing I could *always* leave. That indecision cost me, for I finally found the way out I kept seeking! I should never have assumed discipleship if I didn't intend to stay, whatever reasons arose to encourage my departure! Not unconditionally committing myself was really disastrous!

Nevertheless, my illusion was that I trusted men unworthy of confidence, who knew they would break their word, and did! I believed rabbi an artifice only to embrace the leadership's deception: men who prefer the nation ruined to their profit than the nation preserved to their loss! What reprehensible creatures I trusted. They deserve any malediction imposed!

The treachery of the Sanhedrin is to be blamed, not my sincere effort to effect reconciliation between them and rabbi. They used me merely to seize him, so I'm really the pawn between leaders who demanded deference and a man too proud to submit! I'm victimized by a struggle between a powerful man and a more powerful bureaucracy! I thought I could control my fate by influencing rabbi's—an impossibility I now know! It was out of my control from the first; they planned to kill him two years ago; and, at the end, out of his! We were both subject to unmanageable destinies!

How regrettable that God consigned me to such a tragic role! I wanted more and deserved better. God, why did you let me get involved with this man? Oh, I never dreamed my life would come to this. I thought my decision would lead me to renown in Israel, but never did I think it would lead to this horrifying garbage-dump canyon! What am I doing here sitting here, above the stench? How appropriate for my life right now!! I have never felt such dismal melancholia!

In a mournfully sad way, both rabbi and the Sanhedrin treated me shabbily, using me till I exhausted my usefulness, then discarding me like broken pottery. Either party could have spared me the horrible guilt I've come to feel, for I had the welfare of both at heart, but neither thought of me in their concentration on each other. The Sanhedrin will always have their defenders. If I know the disciples, so will rabbi. But who will defend me? Who will be gracious enough to say that I had good motives. That if my *intentions* had been faithfully executed, my *action* would have been justified? That if rabbi had merely defended himself, or the leaders had kept their promise, my decision would have been heroic, not sinister; applauded, not denounced!

I'm even willing to accept my share of the blame, if only rabbi and the leaders would accept theirs. But that won't happen. They've left me dangling in disgrace because a scapegoat had to be found. I've learned the bitterest lesson: never trust anyone but yourself! Everyone else will fail you! And never step into the breach when God calls for volunteers! He won't rescue you when you're in trouble for obeying him. He'll deny he sent you. He'll deny even knowing you!

What desolation I feel! What abandonment by God! Rabbi, why didn't you declare yourself king a year ago in Galilee, when you had 15,000 people wild with anticipation from your feeding? Why didn't you seize the opportunity last Sunday—just five long mornings ago when you came into this city with thousands proclaiming you? Why didn't you *become* king then, when opportunity rose to its crest?

Your failures summarize my life, rabbi; I put my faith in you, and you deceived me—and I am horribly deceived and now guilty of betraying you—oh God! Is there any sorrow like mine?

Is there something beyond for me? I can't say, but my sufferings have surely paid for whatever misjudgments I've made. And can the future be worse than the hell I've already experienced trying to understand and believe rabbi, only to find he repaid me with counterfeit dreams! God, I can't believe you've let my life come to this!

Still, even now—and I can't understand it at all—I still venerate the man I also loathe! Hard as I try to convince myself that surely rabbi wasn't so perfect after all, especially if one of his own disciples deserted him, surely my once too-great faith became *justifiably* diminished, not a single explanation has relevance or logic! I cannot help but wonder: have I, after all, committed the greater wrong? How many men of rabbi's giftedness have graced Israel? Who was like him in our generation, and when will his like be seen again? Indeed, when did anyone like him previously appear? Is he the one-of-a-kind, unreproducible personality? If he is, have I defrauded Israel of its fairest chance to regain its destiny among the nations? And if I have, won't mine be the crime of the centuries?

Oh...I can't bear to think of that... it rips my heart to shreds! I couldn't have been so evil. Not I, fair man that I am!

Bittersweet reminiscence now returns to mock my villainy: of how comforted the eleven were with faith in rabbi, and how discomfited *that* made me. I complained that faith enslaved them to the *person* of rabbi, but to whom have my doubts enslaved me? Perhaps I should have lectured my disappointments instead of their hope, and chided my assumptions instead of their certainty. Perhaps I should have embraced their faith and denied my cynicism. For what has disputation left me? I'm a shorn lamb, isolated, friendless and disconsolate!

Should I have taken less counsel from my inclinations and more from rabbi's possibilities? Yes, I'm an expert in disputing faith with reason, in alloying faith with speculations, but who wants the cynicism, depression and hopelessness they've brought me? How could I so insolently trust my doubts as evidence of rabbi's fallibility? For myself I speak, and for no one else at all...if I had known what it would eventually cost to doubt, I would have paid the price to believe! For what answers has my betrayal revealed that my discipleship couldn't?

Yes, I got my revenge on him, and on those who trusted him, but how useless to me! I took away their hope, while I punished my disappointment, but how has it benefited me? What have any of us gained by wagering our futures on a rabbi who promised so much, but delivered so little? Have we not all discovered only fear and loss? Are any of the eleven superior to me tonight? Aren't they all scattered, saving their own skins as I'm contemplating suicide?

Still, why did I question their capacity for discernment, but not mine for doubt-inducing questions? We all saw something special in rabbi, but how could I have interpreted it so differently from the eleven? Why did they stay and I bolt? Did we all see only what we pleased, ignoring the contradictions?

Maybe, like them, I should have allowed teacher's mystery to encourage rather than depress me. If I had gone beyond the surface confusion rabbi brought, I might have found explanations in his depths! If he gave me enough reasons to question him, didn't he give many more to trust?

Why did they obey what they *could* believe while I demanded answers to everything as a condition of belief? I used to think that my initial mistake was in failing to follow rabbi with John and Andrew. But now, I wonder...was my initial mistake that I refused to accept by faith the first teachings and perspectives I didn't understand? Didn't my readiness to dispute points of difference develop a habit of disputation with everything rabbi said and did, even where I had no particular argument with it?

Perhaps skepticism's penalty in my life wasn't only to curtail immediate obedience, but to abolish *intention* to obey! It served not only to deny immediate truth, but to lead me to a progressive unconcern for truth until, in self-will, I *rejected* truth and ultimately accepted Sanhedrin *lies* as truth!

Could I have changed my course had I paid the price? Would it have been any higher than the price I'm now going to pay? Did I allow my doubts to deceive me so gradually they eventually eclipsed me completely, now to self-destruction?—a conclusion I can't face and abhor!

Oh, for those early days to come again...when I lived as a child trusting rabbi...before I grew more sophisticated and learned to demand answers and explanations...before I learned to question and deny and become cynical and hard. Oh, to go back and to step out of the boat with Simon...to marvel at teacher's exorcisms and miracles...to gladly receive the answers God gives and to leave the rest to his wisdom...to delight in calling rabbi, "Master," to be at peace because I loved him so! Gone, GONE the days I would love to experience just once more! Too late, too late! I'm recruiting strength I don't have to seek help I can't find! The mistake is irretrievably made, and judgment has come! I'm sickened, bludgeoned and demoralized!

Why...can I state my reasons but justify nothing about the betrayal?

I need to punish myself for what happened—my life for rabbi's. People will say I could do no less, but how could I do more? I deprived him of life; he deprived me of hope. Who did whom the greater wrong, I can't say, but my life for his offers a fair exchange! Jesus dies an innocent man, true to himself; I die a good man, true to my ideals. Surrendering my life removes any guilt in betraying him!

And if, when we both turn to dust and our ashes are mingled, could anyone distinguish between the man many considered their *hope* and the man who found him *wanting*? In time, both of us may well be forgotten, or remembered only for trying to save Israel according to our individual lights.

* * * * *

Morning hinted its arrival in that unfrequented area of the Hinnom Valley. Wildflowers poured perfume Judas didn't smell and birds songs he didn't hear.

He felt so absolutely and uselessly forlorn he knew he had to get away from it all... **IMMEDIATELY...PERMA-NENTLY...,** leaving his wretchedness for what he felt had to be better than the agony he experienced. Who knew what lay ahead, but could it be worse, and who cared anyway since he no longer had reason to live! Indeed, he could explain his betrayal, but could never be at peace with it!

A low-hanging oak branch served his purpose. He moved a stone there, stood on it, removed the cord from his waist, fixed it into a noose, flung the loose end over the limb, then tightened it to the branch. He pulled the noose over his head, snugged it against his throat, then noticed that the branch was thinner than first thought. He pulled hard against it, and decided it was strong enough for his purpose. "Won't hold me for long," he muttered, "but it doesn't have to. They'll probably find me splattered all over the ground, so what does it matter?"

He turned his head upward. "God, I'm giving my life in exchange for rabbi's; it's all I can do, or anyone could; an even match, man for man." He then pulled the noose tightly around his neck and rolled the stone just enough to let him hang freely.

The finality of which found him kicking frantically to once again reach it, legs flailing, seeking its safety, both hands clawing at his neck, trying to escape asphyxiation, reaching the stone with his sandal only to roll it away pawing for it, still snatching at the cloth, striking it anywhere, hoping to jerk it aside until he could reach the rock.

Neck twisting grotesquely, eyes bulging hideously, he gagged at puffs of breath that expelled undistinguished, dying sounds escaping collapsing lungs as he violently swung himself at the stone, but missed altogether. Until, in a few seconds, the clawing grew less and less, the stillness grew more and more, and he soon hung silent, a solitary figure swaying, quite dead, hands askew, fingers out towards his neck, right index finger barely touching it, intentionally alone in death as he had so often inexcusably felt himself alone in life!

Wanderers later found the result—Judas was right about that tree branch being lighter than he first thought. The glaring sun bloated his body, it broke the branch, and down it came, its rupture gushing repulsive fluids that wild dogs consumed, leaving so little no one could identify the remains. They found the disciples' money bag in the garment's blood-soaked pocket, with so little in it they first thought him a beggar. Then they

saw a name stitched into the collar of the garment, sewn by a
man too proud to die unknown, but not humble enough to
practice the self-denial that rendered suicide unnecessary.

They took the bag and gave it to the authorities. All fuss
and feathers, they immediately pronounced it just punishment
for such a scoundrel, then hastily purchased the plot of ground
as a burial place. That's all Judas gained by his treachery: a
field useless to any purpose but a graveyard in which the dis-
honored dead— unknown paupers, foreigners and
vagrants—would rot unnoticed and unattended!

What a *long* way from his dreams Judas died! How far
from his schemes of wealth and grandeur! How near the
infamy in which he would be eternally damned!

The same day Judas' body burst open, another body burst
OUT. Resurrecting himself. From the dead! Exiting the
grave! Through an open tomb! Alive forevermore! Jesus
Christ! God over all! Forever praised! Rendering cemeteries
OBSOLETE!

PART IV

SPIRITUAL PRINCIPLES JUDAS OVERLOOKED

THE VALUE OF COMMUNITY LIFE OVER PERSONAL EXPERIENCE

Being the only Judean among the Twelve, Judas felt superior to the Galileans he irritably censured for indiscriminately trusting Jesus. When he learned that sharing his reservations led to disputation, he kept his own counsel, further isolating him from the others and elevating himself to infallible judge. Putting Jesus on trial whenever he disagreed, Judas demanded evidence he never thought sufficient once given, and nourished doubts he never considered unfair, however flagrant. He flatly rejected an axiomatic Bible truth: we can lack understanding of God without taking offense with him; we can be confused by God without losing faith in him.

Like the third servant in the Parable of the Talents, who believed only he understood the lord, Judas trusted only his appraisal of Christ. Like Thomas, he kept his skepticism private, embracing any cause as an excuse to doubt. Like Philip, he didn't mature in discipleship, but continued to filter every activity and teaching through the perspectives of a fiery patriot demanding a political and military reign. He never contemplated spiritual laws creating their own rules, even when individuals and governments considered them irrelevant.

While a number of factors attracted Judas to Jesus, only one concentrated his attention: Jesus as Messiah addressing contemporary issues: Roman taxes, occupation and usurpation. However successful in other ways, Jesus had to resolve those issues to retain Judas' interest.

The Twelve shared the national assumption—not surprising given the combination of secular and sacred roles Moses and David filled. Since Messiah would be Moses' successor and David's son, tradition demanded he assume their dual responsibilities, directing national life while priests functioned according to the Law.

The mind set didn't doom Judas. *Personalizing* the nation in himself, determining that Jesus failed the nation by failing him, doomed Judas. As did his equally adamant presumption that Jesus couldn't be *any kind* of Messiah if not a political Messiah—a presumption none of the eleven shared!

When Judas finally decided that Jesus lacked the truculence characteristic of *his* messianic profile—whose shrill, primeval summons to war would recruit armies and destroy Rome—he fumed that Jesus failed him! And if Jesus proved inadequate to human need, should it surprise him that mortals, with their prejudices and predilections, to say nothing of their native intelligence, would reject him?

To convince himself that no one else in Israel had ever scrimmaged with God's will, Judas ignored the ample testimony of her sacred books. Had he thought about it, the Psalms explode with provocative exclamations of the despair he felt. An unsounded depth of candid skepticism lurked there, contesting the often-irreconcilable discrepancy between faith and God's inscrutability in distress! The visceral suspicion surfaced by Job's ghastly suffering also testified, confronting those in every age who believe in God, yet freely question his appalling unconcern just when they need him most! And what of the contention Abraham, Moses, David and Jeremiah expressed!

When Judas protested that he heard everything Jesus said, but found it defied his personal experience, he hadn't been alone! The perplexities experienced by the ancients counseled his, for they had all doubted God's concern and questioned his promises when they experienced neither! Instead, where the national literature ultimately admitted human frailty and God's mystery, Judas postulated human infallibility and God's insufficiency!

Unlike those believers, who experienced temporary isolation from God, or anger towards God, Judas ultimately repudiated God. Judas knew the exact worth of perfume but not the value of persevering *faith* where personal experience failed! Self-absorbed, he couldn't empathize with the eleven, or put himself in their place, or broaden his view by submitting it to theirs or, when needing reinforcement of his confidence and convictions, yield himself to their influence! He would never let their assurance discipline his incredulity.

Expecting acknowledgment from, he never offered it to them. Demanding that they prove themselves to him, he considered himself above proof. Insatiably hungry for applause from the many he considered his inferiors, the few he considered his peers and the only one he had once considered his superior, Judas never felt moved to offer praise for effort and kudos for achievement. Anyone relating to him had to reinforce his self-esteem though, paradoxically, reinforcement invariably buttressed his insecurity, giving him further cause for contempt. His sorrows grew with every effort at reducing them, his burdens with every effort at lightening them. He fell victim to misperceptions he wouldn't *have* corrected because he felt them unanswerable!

Like the Dwarfs in *The Chronicles of Narnia*, Judas trusted Judas and no one else, and that became a prodigious, if unintended, multiplier of his disaffection! With self-absorption came self-pity that soared when the instant gratification he craved returned unsatisfied, or when he felt himself overlooked, demeaned or disappointed—as he never failed to *be*, even if he had to create it in his own mind, *which he faithfully did*!

He always ran from the truth that challenged to the deception that soothed. That led him to eventually become a confirmed hater of the only true friend he ever had, who would have forgiven his many failures to reinforce his few successes.

We know exactly how he began his march to infamy. Forgetting the law of the echo, when he couldn't resolve what he considered discrepancies between his absolutes and Christ's temporizing, Judas began a gradual mental and spiritual journey from Jesus, losing his conscience one event at a time, his conviction one experience at a time and his commitment one decision at a time. In almost unnoticed ways he lost the faith he once held *until* one day it vanished, and he couldn't find it, however he tried. Until he didn't care if he lost it and no longer wanted to find it at all.

What we don't know is why he continued that march, when the combined witness of 1500 years, and the steadfastness of the eleven, warned him from it! And if he *could* convince himself that the ancients didn't relate to his situation, he couldn't deny the testimony of eleven men! They shared all his confusion when facing Christ, but none of his bitter response.

Never had they known a person simultaneously so intimate and distant; accessible and remote; permissive and strict; mortal and infinite; historic and eternal, a person they could neither deny nor explain...unimpeachably human, unimpeachably divine. Confronted by his mystery, they remained loyal only by exercising the possibilities implied by his presence instead of the limitations imposed by their conjectures. That explains why, where the eleven saw lightning in Christ's life, Judas felt only the paralyzing bolt! For where Jesus allowed access to their probing *faith*, he denied access to Judas' sullen *suspicion*.

Not that Jesus didn't raise enough issues to dispute if someone looked for a quarrel. Still, eleven men remained faithful to him, despite their questions, and one betrayed because of his. He refused the testimony of men certainly his peers and, as events proved, his spiritual superiors. Against their overwhelming loyalty to Jesus he revolted! He rebelled not only against Christ himself, but against other mortals in the same group Jesus had convinced! Since the entity always exceeds the sum of its parts, the total faith of the eleven compensated for Judas' lack of spiritual substance. He could have been saved from himself had he accepted tutoring from the *community grace* that saved them from themselves.

Judas wouldn't accept Christ's truth, then, because he refused to *persevere* in faith. "Judas *shared* in this ministry," Peter said in **Acts 1:17**, without *continuing* in it; admitting his original place while denouncing his ultimate fate! A fate he deserved because he refused to escape it!

Christians would be better critics of his behavior but for our frequent repetition of it; and brighter scholars of his pedagogy if we learned from instead of imitating it. Like Judas, we've ignored what columnist William Safire calls the Rule of Holes: when in one, stop digging. Like him, we continue reinforcing behaviors that weaken our spiritual security.

DEMANDING EVIDENCE

The Judas Complex flares in us every time we wonder why God can't make his existence *so obvious* no one can dissent!

Two inconsistencies mar that swill. One, there isn't a scientist alive who doesn't welcome *mystery* in the natural world as essential to *learning*. Yet, these same people demand definitive answers to all spiritual questions before they believe in God. They consistently accept mystery in creation, then inconsistently demand a transparent Creator!

Two, the lament of the skeptic, "Give us more evidence, God, make yourself CLEAR," merely renews the request of the Jewish leadership in **John 10:24**, "How long will you keep us in suspense? If you are the Christ, tell us plainly." His evidence by then included exorcised demons, resurrected dead and thousands fed, healed and restored, to say nothing of nonpareil teachings. Yet, *seeing* him before them, they demanded more of the same, though they rejected all the previous! Where did the fault lie, then: in Christ's transmission or their receptors?

The second blast of Mt. St. Helens May, 1980 could be heard 200 miles away, but not by a film crew four miles away! Like that film crew, people don't see the evidence God offers because they position themselves where they can't, then foolishly conclude he hasn't offered any!

PERSEVERING IN EVIL BEHAVIOR

We as naturally seek destructive behaviors as we reluctantly relinquish them once embraced, despite the appeal of concerned Christian friends. When their persevering holiness mocks our dereliction, we change companions instead of habits, substituting conscientious with accommodating friends!

WEAKENING UNDER ADVERSITY

We quickly lose our spiritual audacity, and surface controversy over God's promises when suffering disappointment, pain or loss. Every believer, including those in whom faith's pulse beats strongest, can fall into anguished skepticism over God's apparent disregard of them, altering discipleship from anchored absolutes to drifting equivocation: "do I really believe this?"

FORGETTING INDIVIDUAL WEAKNESS

We mistakenly exalt our personal over the faith community's accumulated experience. The problem originates in the *awareness* of *individuality* created in every conception and publicizes itself in the disparity between community teaching and our personal life. In the difference we instinctively declare only our erudition valid!—a fault Satan delightfully exploits, knowing that God won't offer evidence to prove something about himself or to retain our discipleship. Viewing human depravity, the unsaved raise objections when we declare God's mercy. Experiencing spasms of adversity, believers often question their own affirmations about God's concern. Suddenly, sometimes subtly, sometimes blatantly, the Judas Complex questions, "where does truth exist if I can't find it in my life?"

The faith-experience necessarily walks alone against the flesh-experience. That's the inevitable and unavoidable "narrow" versus "broad" way Jesus set before us. But *within* the faith-experience, the church's time-tested adventure can sustain us when misfortune has mangled our own. The Judas Complex declares, "If it hasn't happened to me, it can't be real for you." The community rejoins, "The body of Christ says it's true, even if it hasn't yet happened to you, and maybe never will."

We can rationally and wisely trust the accumulated experience of the *body*! Any Biblical congregation holds a surfeit of the spiritual patrimony individual Christians may neglect, overlook or misplace; and exhibits a credibility individual experience can't disregard. The church's testimony carries us like luggage when we want to drop out because God hasn't answered our personal prayers and expectations! When God's word and personal experience don't agree, discriminating Christians take refuge in the expansive competence of God's people, not in their own narrow experience! The cumulative success of his kingdom's 3500 years balances, corrects and disciplines our 60-80 years!

To seek in others the answers we sometimes don't personally have demands unaccustomed humility, but is pride worth ignorance and failure? Individual Christians should openly discuss their questions and reservations with godly, Christ-honoring disciples. While we're individually no stronger or wiser when facing difficulties, in the united strength of the body, joined with the church through the ages, exists and exudes a power that terrifies Satan, because he can't withstand it, and from which he keeps trying to divert us, because it destroys his influence over us!

QUESTIONING GOD HIMSELF

Faith in God can tolerate, outlast and overcome doubts that rise over adverse circumstances or God's decisions and declarations. But questioning God himself—his nature and intentions—preys on faith like wolves on the flock. Faith demands both a knowledge of God's word and the acknowledgment of God's presence! And objective belief in God's existence must fashion and correct subjective faith. Without that objective reality, subjective confidence is all too easily faith in illusion! Christians: distrust in the person of God lurks like Banquo's ghost in every believer, a treachery not only always possible, but often expressed in our terrors!

MAINTAINING OUR ERRORS

False suppositions and inadequate opinions are expected in recent converts. What maturing Christian can't laugh over erroneous and silly past persuasions?

It's as we continue to insist on our views that discipleship fails. Christ's word assayed all his listeners, proving their spiritual worth. What he said made absolutely no sense to some. Others responded by impulse, but quickly withered. Some, and in this category I think we find Judas, responded sincerely while preserving convictions that became debris competing with and eventually choking Christ's truth.

God's word can't compete with either tradition or the unconverted allegiances imported to and welcomed as equals of faith. Both mistakes invariably review and judge new input by established prejudices that insist on subjection! And though we're to blame when God's word fails to satisfy or cleanse or enable us, the convictions, persuasions and prejudices of our unconverted self excoriate God. As Solomon said, "A man's folly ruins his life, yet he rages against the Lord," **Proverbs 19:3**. That's why Jesus demanded *self-denial*, so even the self that will stand in the way if we let it can become the servant of, not the master of grace.

* * * * *

To develop the manpower needed when constructing their innovative 777, Boeing Aircraft executives established revolutionary teamwork. Anyone involved in the construction could freely admit having problems. The group would discuss the issue and, using the company's massed wisdom in aircraft manufacturing, resolve it before work continued.

Since church leaders make poor innovators, they should at least be better imitators! They must assure members that: it's okay to have doubts about God and frustrations with God; it's all part of mastering a perfect faith in a fallen world; they shouldn't become estranged from the church when it happens; the nurturing atmosphere of the body will support them in their turmoil; they won't be forsaken or criticized; the *community's* unmeasured spiritual resources will offer the hope they lack to overcome the despair they feel until the faith they've misplaced returns.

In *Pilgrim's Progress,* Hopeful discovered that help. On the Enchanted Ground he grew so weary he wanted only to sleep. An alert Christian urged him instead to remember the Shepherd's earlier warning of the danger posed by the Enchanted Ground: "we should beware of sleeping; wherefore 'let us not sleep, as do others; but let us watch and be sober'" **I Thessalonians 5:6**.

Hopeful accepted the encouragement, admitting, "I acknowledge myself in a fault; and had I been here alone, I had by sleeping run the danger of death."

As we all do when we feel alone in our spiritual experience! By belonging to the group we lose the sense of isolation that easily destroys faith! That's why, when we find ourselves weakening in or falling from faith, we should flee to the group, whose faith-net catches us. In the visible community of believers, as in the invisible concourse of those dead in faith, exists laughter that dries our tears; the presence of millions that banishes isolation; and the testimony of God's people that verifies the unimpeachable truth his word reveals and imposes, whatever our momentary personal experience may say! Only what we exercise grows, whether gifts, skills, faith or doubt. In regard to faith in Christ, will we *exercise* the doubt of the one man or the faith of the eleven?

THE NECESSITY OF FAITH IN DISCIPLESHIP

The wonder isn't that one betrayed Jesus and eleven remained faithful, but that **only** one grew disillusioned enough to betray. With the others, Judas had once believed Jesus a true prophet. Then he began to be surprised by what he heard, then shocked, then uncomfortable, then skeptical, then finally hardened against Christ. Refusing to trust the MAN Jesus, Judas soon depreciated his teaching, leading him to unconcern for truth, to rejection of truth and ultimate acceptance of lies as truth!

The eleven distinguished themselves from Judas by a superior faith in, not by a superior comprehension of Jesus. By retaining child-like faith they dramatized an unlimited ability to morph from sinner to saint. Judas, ever the philosopher, and addicted to the *search* for knowledge, accepted only what his reason judged reasonable. He began with their potential, but forfeited it because he refused to subordinate his interrogations to trust; until Jesus could no longer hoist any flag Judas would salute and found each mentally dismantled by Judas as he raised them. That mind set first limited his ability to grow, then hastened his rush to estrangement from into betrayal of Christ.

If the Twelve had been canvassed, each would admit to frustration with Christ. Yet, if they had been canvassed, all but one trusted him. And only one admitted disenchantment with and alienation from Jesus *because* he couldn't understand him. In the last year of Christ's ministry Judas remained the Satan he had became a year before, though during that time Jesus offered some of his most dramatic teachings and miracles. He wouldn't let that year's evidence convince his previous eighteen months of denial! In those months he brushed doubt as the HMS Titanic brushed the iceberg—with equally disastrous results. The difference was it took Judas a year to sink!

The distinction between human limitations and God's infinity threatens faith only when we demand unlimited freedom for our limitations and limitations on God's infinity. *Then* doubts and disputes become questions, not about God's decisions and declarations, but about God himself. Trust is the foundation of our relationship with God. Without it, unhappy, unfair, undeserved circumstances will threaten and demolish us. Since crisis isn't the best time to learn trust in God, he insists we begin our discipleship in faith, and continue in faith all the time—so when hard times come we'll be in the *habit*! And hard times will come. The Bible assumes it; Jesus teaches it; human experience verifies it! Satan assures a surfeit of opportunities to doubt God! Only systematic anchoring by faith will keep us from drifting away!

If Judas had understood that possibility, he wouldn't have let his darker side contaminate faith, and wouldn't have allowed reservations about Jesus' teachings and methods to erode confidence in the Lord himself. Indeed, he would have understood the impossibility of comprehending Jesus. Others remained faithful by trusting his evidence. By refusing to trust, Judas twisted Christ's proofs into reproofs. As a result, what proved temporary setbacks for the eleven proved permanent defeats for him. What dealt them stinging rebuttals dealt him fatal blows. Only he carried all their feelings, disappointments and sorrows into rabid rejection of the *Man* from Galilee.

Judas ultimately learned that doubt went far beyond a mere statement of fact just as the eleven learned that faith went beyond a mere statement of hope. Both led to conclusions and lifestyles. No question that Jesus made it hard for his men to trust, with his enigmatic teachings and bold, colossal claims. *Then*...demanded faith as the means by which they could be sure of him and have their doubts resolved! Amazing audacity! Yet the eleven found the risk only in the initial effort, not in the after-experience. By refusing the initial effort Judas doomed himself to the after-experience, which he came to loathe. It kept him busy explaining to himself how *he* couldn't be wrong, and had to be right, and Jesus couldn't be right and had to be wrong! And that not only weakened his capacity for discipleship but undermined the possibility of discipleship, for no one can be a persevering disciple who disputes with his Maker!

Speaking of Mary Magdalene's inability to recognize Christ at the tomb, George MacDonald wrote that even the most excusable, unavoidable doubt blinds the doubter to God's presence. Practiced unbelief blinded Judas!

Judas' failure teaches us to persevere in *faith*, to seek visions that enlarge it, testings that challenge it, tasks that build it and promises that encourage it! For Satan intends to make forsaking God easy and staying with God hard! He seeks to lead from God any who will follow him away and to dissuade the rest from considering God! And he does his work most effectively by insinuating God's ineffectiveness in crisis, God's unapproachability due to our sinfulness, God's unconcern in our needs.

Judas never felt that **Jesus** proved definitively convincing. Where the eleven learned to trust **Jesus** from listening and watching, Judas never learned to trust him at all, though listening and watching with them! He always needed more proof! Yet, if *seeing* the Son of God weren't adequate evidence, what would be? If watching him at work couldn't develop faith, what could? When exposure to God's word stills interrogators—and we continue to question, the *desire* to believe is wanting, not belief itself. And *desire* can be gained only by conversion, not by producing more evidence.

What a denunciation to bear! Judas wouldn't offer Jesus the trust he demanded from every disciple. *That* Judas refused. No mantle of discipleship would he wear if, in wearing it, he had to absolutely trust the One who demanded faith in the unseen, in what he didn't understand at all and confidence that the MYSTERY WRITER had the right to keep the secrets he wished when revealing the mysteries he pleased.

He rejected the faith that energized for the skepticism that exhausted him! That led him to savage Jesus when he didn't explain, and to cavil with him when he did. Despising the refusal, he despised any explanation! Judas would put his head in the noose complaining that God hadn't answered his questions as a means of gaining his trust.

Skeptics and Christians continue the battle over evidence that Judas and the eleven began. Skeptics claim we believe despite inadequate evidence; we say they doubt despite overwhelming evidence. Skeptics think we can't believe by accepting evidence they deny. We refuse to disbelieve just because they deny evidence we accept.

Skeptics say that anyone can believe, but can faith be sustained by evidence many consider insufficient? Christians reply that anyone can deny, but can doubt be sustained when confronted by evidence that infinitely many more consider redundant? They say we believe despite questions that clearly leave doubt; we say they doubt despite facts that clearly demand faith.

The same evidence exists, prompting distinctive responses: skeptics refusing to believe until more of their questions are answered; Christians devotedly believing because the important ones already are!

As the life of Judas proved, perspective, not evidence is at fault! Human pride keeps us *believing* that God's proofs haven't reached our evidentiary threshold. And, mistakenly seeing argument as the highest expression of intelligence, people indefatigably argue with God!

However, another fact needs to be stressed. Neither believers nor skeptics can be trusted to be objective. Whatever evidence we affirm or they deny, all that either may prove is personal predilection: we to believe, they to doubt. Since neither skeptics nor we have any impact on the *production* of evidence, the determination of evidentiary sufficiency comes from God! Without asking our affirmation or denial, God has given the evidence **he** thought necessary to reach the informed decision he declares essential about Jesus Christ. And while God frequently hides his *providence* in difficult circumstances, to test faith, he always reveals *evidence* to create faith!

The great, unanswerable evidence for faith is Jesus Christ alive from the dead—because his bodily resurrection is indisputable and demands acceptance! If he hadn't risen, skeptics are right and Christians shouldn't play at "religion" by worshiping a man who is dust! But since he alone of all historical personalities has risen from the dead, skeptics are wrong and should admit it, whether or not they intend to accept him as Lord and Savior. For it isn't honest to deny his resurrection just because we refuse to commit our lives to him!

Faith as surely exists without apology as unbelief without excuse, but all that is beside the point! If we don't want Jesus ruling us, tell him so, and he'll grant our request. He won't go where he isn't wanted and won't stay where he isn't welcomed!

But don't use specious arguments against his bodily resurrection to hide pride and self-will. That's sheer hypocrisy!

Last of all, *faith* offers the final appeal of both believers and skeptics. They *believe* the evidence is insufficient, we *believe* it's overflowing! Both go ultimately with *faith*—unbelievers don't have a higher law or power! One group **believes** the evidence; the other **disbelieves** the evidence! And **Hebrews 10:38** reveals God's response to both: "But my righteous one will live by faith. And if he shrinks back, I will not be pleased with him."

CHRIST'S RIGHT TO DEFINE HIS KINGDOM

Little wonder that our culture has refined arrogance to an art; we've been practicing it since Eden, where Eve made our first and worst mistake. God had specifically warned Adam that eating the fruit from the Tree of the Knowledge of God and Evil would bring death. **Nevertheless**, Eve thought the fruit offered *wisdom*! Her opinion against God's word, a tradition we slavishly continue.

Nevertheless, God provides in Christ the gifts we seek only when we accept Christ as the GIFT he's given! Jesus Christ is the all-sufficient personality who renders other personalities footnotes to his life! We can get advice from any religious leader, but only he gives help. Another will tell us something pleasant, but he tells us something necessary, pleasant or not. Another will tell us what we want to hear, he what we need to know!

That foundational sufficiency makes Jesus either a benefactor or a threat to all who confront him. When he takes what we want to lose, we love him as a benefactor; when he takes what we want to keep, we fear him as a threat. In a society that seeks a religious cuff to the emotions, but not a spiritual wallop to the head, people satisfy themselves with a "feel good" experience. They abhor the spiritual authority that distinguishes between true and false religion, true and false doctrine, true and false life and true and false discipleship!

People who love artifice and embrace illusion practice self-assertion, self-fulfillment and self-realization—terms they use to postulate their intention to *remain in charge* of life—consider Jesus a threat because he demands self-denial. Those who have tired of the lying gurus, and their emphasis on human potential and the "god-within", see Jesus as a benefactor because he tells the truth, especially when he says, "You're what's keeping God from loving you and including you in his kingdom...*give yourself up!*"

Whatever our opinions or desires, the Christian faith isn't a Rorschach test, with us determining its interpretation and application—and each acceptable, even if contradictory! Jesus Christ retains complete authority over his kingdom, though we've never stopped disputing him or pitting our opinion against his word. We seem to think that God can exist only as we define him; and that we can willingly admit our sins because we can also dictate the terms of forgiveness!

Even those renewed in Christ's image sometimes unconsciously maintain the fiction of our authority in God's church, particularly seen in the struggle between traditionalists and innovators over church growth. Both posit the truth of their opinion and suspiciously eye the other's.

Traditionalists regularly state the ten most dangerous words in the English language: "We want to grow, but we don't want to change." An oxymoron, since life is a matter of constant change! Only change allows growth since, as Bob Kelly said, the same people doing the same things in the same way produces the **same** results! Church members can so faithfully serve God that they fail to see beyond their own experience; they lose spiritual objectivity by religious involvement. By resisting change in methodology, they invariably keep churches under their personal control–Diotrophes like. These good people *seek* growth, but only within their comfort level.

However, the church growth movement runs two significant dangers. The first is to become so aware of what people want to hear that we don't teach what God wants them to know! We can pique people's interest without converting them! The divine TEACHER still retains the right to say what his students need to learn and never gives them power over his curriculum!

Second, the greatest danger posed by the church growth movement is the intentional freedom leaders give members and friends. It's the declared rule in such churches: provide many opportunities for Bible study and other involvement, but let individuals determine how involved they'll get, in what and where! The unspoken assumption is that individual Christians get the option of determining how deep in faith they'll go and grow!

However, as **Ephesians 2:10** teaches, each new Christian's destiny is already established. Spiritual perfection, which Jesus models, is always our goal! Towards it we always move; closer to it we must be as time passes. Church-growth churches must perforce stress higher discipleship *expectations.* And, to build into Christians a depth they haven't reached, leaders must teach at a depth they've never heard! Above all, leaders must teach that our purpose as believers isn't to be an *improved,* but a *converted* humanity. Our goal isn't to *upgrade* self but to *renew* it in Christ's likeness! Just as Jesus determines how we become Christians he determines our lifestyle afterwards! We don't figure in either decision!

Jesus also outlines the personnel parameters of his kingdom. Nowhere did he more powerfully impact that future than in choosing women and children as chief beneficiaries of his esteem. Consider the Samaritan woman. Offered a love he alone possessed, and as freely gave, she surrendered to it, and quickly shared with others. Jesus offered two defining principles in that interview. One, his appeal would be universal. Two, his appeal, once accepted, would be heralded. The woman reacted instinctively to her new life, sharing her faith with the same townspeople from whom she had long been alienated. She forgot the 10,000 excuses that *clamored* for silence for the single reason that *whispered* for testimony!

In extolling children as model kingdom citizens, Jesus outlined the definitive trait children possess in abundance: their trust in people who love them! The person's looks, color, nationality, religion, anonymity mean nothing if they exude love and concern. Assured of that, children leave everything else to faith!

The eleven felt like little children in Christ's presence! John, and likely all but Judas felt comfortable putting his head on Christ's chest—like a little boy snuggling to his dad! Judas wouldn't humiliate himself so; he felt independent of everyone, even of Jesus. A male in a society that honored males; a grown man in a society that demanded responsibility from grown men, he wouldn't tolerate less. If he had to accept the responsibility of adulthood, he demanded its prerogatives: the privilege of thinking for himself, choosing for himself, determining right from wrong in any teacher he heard, how far that teacher's influence would impact him and how far his discipleship would extend! Judas would never understand that all who come to God are his *children*, not his *adults.*

Judas' attitude has been adapted by many in history, particularly intellectuals who love *knowledge*. They continue the debate that Erasmus and Luther surfaced in the Reformation. Erasmus said: let men think; Luther replied: let God speak. Erasmus said: since we think, let reason be our guide; Luther responded: since God has spoken, obey him! While Christians continue to stress faith in God's evidence, humanists say they want to KNOW, not believe! And that includes questions of religion. If they can't **KNOW** there's a God, they refuse to **BELIEVE** in him.

How insane! The stupidest thing we'll ever do is to demand from God what he has warned us from the beginning he'll *never* provide. When they could with Christians **believe** for this life—for we live by faith, not by sight; and **know** for the next—for then we shall know, even as we are fully known, they'll spend eternity **believing**! And this is what they'll believe: they'll BELIEVE it's all a mistake that they'll never KNOW anything again!

God will never betray himself to win us, encourage us or convince us! There is no stronger-willed person in history than Jesus Christ! And when he declared that faith in him as the Son of God was the essential without which no discipleship could exist, he accepted nothing less. It was stupid of Judas to ever think Jesus would bow to his will; it's stupid of anyone making his mistake today. Any demand we make that contradicts God's word will mock, accuse and torment us!

It's true, as Pascal says, "We are given enough light for those to see who only desire to see; and enough obscurity for those who have a contrary disposition." However, while God gives us enough light to see, and enough obscurity to keep us blind, he *never* gives us influence in his kingdom! Skeptics hate that! We so cleverly re-create the lives of the ancients, and so powerfully impact our current history that we feel capable of determining the future life! And that damned egotism will cast us into Hell!

The God who owes us nothing, and gives us everything, alone defines his kingdom, whether we dispute him, deny him or accept him. He doesn't reign at our sufferance. Our acceptance doesn't give him permission he wouldn't otherwise have, or freedom he'd otherwise be denied. It merely qualifies us to receive his grace.

We should submit to Christ's rule immediately and unreservedly. Now, while we *can* say no, but say yes. While we *can* refuse, but assent. While we're standing, but *fall* in submission. Whatever our doubts, we should come to God; whatever our reservations, we should come to God. The poorest reason for accepting Christ excels the best reason for rejecting him.

The battle between Christ's dominion and our pretense continues — the unresolved issue between the Savior and the sinners he died to save. And, as America's religious portfolio diversifies it becomes harder to convince our culture of the Savior's singularity. Jesus as one of the great religious leaders poses no problems to many. But Jesus as the Only way to God is intolerant, they say.

Their problem! The Bible is adamant; Christianity alone has a living, historical leader alive in his time, dead for the specific purpose of forgiving sins, bodily alive the third day to justify faith in all his previous teachings and miracles, ascended into Heaven, sitting at God's Right Hand — and coming again in ineffable Glory! We must deal with **him** — on *his* terms, not ours!

ONLY GOD'S GRACE CAN EFFECT REPENTANCE

By returning the money Judas openly confessed Christ's innocence and unwittingly admitted his mistake in betraying him. But he hadn't repented.

Given his mind set, he never could. Godly sorrow comes from betrayal of God, not self; of his standards, not ours. Selfishly sorrowful, Judas regretted only that the failure embarrassed him! Judas had a distorted view of wrongdoing. For him, as for many Jewish legalists, sin had been encoded in law, categorizing it. Wrongdoing was no longer spiritual, but judicial; something to be judicially penalized, not expunged by forgiveness. Infractions galore which judges should punish, but not transgressions God alone could. Thus, acting as his own judge, he committed suicide! And, having penalized himself, felt he paid his debt and deserved no further condemnation.

That had been Judas' problem in discipleship. We can conjecture that he wouldn't seek forgiveness because he hadn't thought he sinned; or because he considered his act too catastrophic to forgive. Either way, by committing suicide, he continued the self-directed, controlling behavior he had always practiced. *He*, not Jesus, would determine his life.

All human mistakes issue from ego–*I know what's best for me!* Judas let human frailty become transgression by refusing to let Christ discipline it.

Judas would have risen above his victories by crediting others; and above his defeats by blaming self. But both contradicted his values. He neither shared credit nor accepted blame. He would necessarily have to tear up his ego by the roots to admit indebtedness to anyone–and that he would never do.

Judas would get what he wanted, even if it meant Jesus had to change his entire focus; or Jesus had to be arrested; or Judas had to commit suicide! For he would rather die trying to have his way than to live with Christ having his! Like Augustine before his conversion, Judas would rather have God overcome by him to his destruction than himself overcome by God to his salvation!

Who can tell where he started that self-destructive lifestyle? It certainly preceded his discipleship. He had been becoming the high chair king long before Jesus called him from it to responsible behavior! *But, why change for rabbi*, Judas conjectured, *when I can alter him; haven't others accommodated me? Why shouldn't Jesus?*

Wherever it started, he indulged his self-centeredness, fed its appetite, massaged its hope, welcomed its imperious presence and enthroned its mandate. Until his ego became a mad dog and he could only let it run, because denying it hurt too much, cost too much and left him subject to others!

When it became obvious that Jesus wouldn't change to accommodate him, Judas struck back as high chair kings do—by denial, refusal, disrespect and contempt. When nothing worked to alter Christ's method and message, Judas knew he had to consult the one power in Israel greater than himself. When the Sanhedrin also victimized him, Judas decided to punish Jesus and Israel for refusing his demands by killing himself. That would show them!

Choosing self-destruction over self-criticism proves how thoroughly his self-love had grown. When Peter found himself threatened with death on the sea, he cried, "Lord, save me!" Judas, on the verge of suicide would never call out, "Lord, save me!" That would have meant he had to look outside himself for help, and he had never done that!

Never...not in Scripture, not in time, not in eternity can we determine how or where we pay for our sins. God alone determines that. Sin is spiritual, not judicial. It can be penalized by law, but removed only by forgiveness—as Jesus taught in **Matthew 18:27**. Sin cannot be removed by a sentence of punishment! Of all the flaws in the theory of Purgatory, this is the most glaring: it says we can escape wrongdoing by being punished. Wrong. We can pay forever for our sins by being punished, but we can never be released from sin by being punished. Release from sin comes only from forgiveness, which originates only in God's grace!

Judas took the coward's way, eliminating himself; not the courageous way, eliminating his sin by having it forgiven! Brave enough to defy God's love in Christ, Judas proved too cowardly to accept the correction that would have restored him to it.

While nothing would have recovered the betrayal's disgrace, Judas, like Peter, Thomas and Saul, could have learned to live with it, glory in it and extol the Savior whose forgiveness could reach even he—an example of grace greater than even *his* sins! But he couldn't face that prospect. Let others live with shame, he said; he wouldn't! No, but he would kill himself to avoid it! Judas simply loved himself too much to repent. He would rather die in shame than live with it!

Had Judas listened carefully, Jesus clearly described repentance in the story of the Prodigal Son. The boy finally realized his pitiful condition as *son* contrasted to his father's *servants*! But he hadn't yet repented, though many consciously feel their desperate condition, and satisfy themselves with grieving over it.

He made a resolution—to go back home and apologize. But he hadn't repented then either—though many make similar promises to God, particularly in desperate circumstances.

He got up and returned to his father. And he hadn't completed his repentance even then, though many think they have when they agree to be baptized.

His repentance began with a conviction and ended with an *action*—the *admission* that he was no longer worthy to be called a son! He wanted back in his father's house even if he imposed penalties for leaving—which the boy expected.

Repentance is complete only when we realize we can make no *claim* on grace because we're useless servants. That humility alone activates God's mercy and stills his wrath! Returning to God involves our acknowledgment of unworthiness to return! Repentance *begins* with an awakening that we've sinned but ends only when we confess that we have no right to confess at all, but only to be punished!

Judas obviously experienced a brutal orgy of self-recrimination before returning the money. But self-flagellation brought no satisfaction, enjoyment or peace because he kept thinking the crime had been against himself, not against

God–and therefore needed proscription, not forgiveness! He mourned in self-pity that led to regret when he could have mourned in godly sorrow leading to release. Had he taken his confession to the cross, Jesus would have forgiven. But he took it only to the Sanhedrin–and what did they care? Guilt of any kind–even against another human—must be first confessed as guilt against God. David underscored that in **Psalm 51:4**. All misbehavior towards other humans reflects our initial rejection of God's presence in life!

Returning to God without that admission may bring us temporary sorrow, but not permanent repentance. It may get us into church membership, but not into the circle of the justified! Christians have been to the funeral of their past, but can never claim they deserved to celebrate escape from death to life, from despair to hope, from guilt to exoneration! We can only realize that the God we inexcusably offended has inexplicably **forgiven** because he loves us so much!

Denial, intrigue, argumentation and self-justification have historically been humanity's response when accused of sinfulness by God, when found guilty of sin by others, when confessing sin ourselves. And so skilled are we in evading reproaches we don't want to bear, and escaping sights we don't want to see, that repentance is often incomplete and flawed, filled with the chicanery, denial and self-justification that blind us to God's grace!

Sadly, Judas tried every expedient but not the truth! He couldn't see either the magnitude of his own sin or the grace that would have reached back had he reached out to it. He kept *himself* in the way. Since self is always in the way when we confront our sins and God's holiness, God puts self to death in repentance—and never wants it alive to torment the new as it did the old person!

INTRUDING OUR WILL
INTO GOD'S WORD
CREATES DEGENERATE
WICKEDNESS

Using Judas and Peter as models, how can we explain that
Jesus anathematized Judas' betrayal and exonerated Simon's
denial? That he uttered malediction on Judas and a prayer for
Simon?

It wasn't because Peter was a Galilean and Judas a Judean,
though Judas would have sworn that. Believers and skeptics
came from both provinces, and the Master's appeal surmounted
all racial, sexual, religious, political, social and geographical
boundaries.

It wasn't because Judas sinned and Simon didn't. Both
denied Jesus that night. Peter's bitter weeping originated in
horrifying *guilt*, not in emotional disturbance.

It wasn't because Judas drew a different conclusion about
Jesus from Peter. Many in Israel who first drew wrong later
drew right conclusions about him, as Saul of Tarsus discovered.

It wasn't because Jesus disliked Judas and liked Peter,
though again Judas would have sworn to it. Jesus welcomed all
those serious about discipleship. Peter and Judas were entirely
different personalities–as contradictory as any two among the
Twelve: Peter provocatively extroverted, Judas nearly invisible;
Peter voluble about, Judas quiet in his convictions; Peter emotionally inconstant, Judas thoughtfully consistent. Peter could
precipitously reach a decision, find it wrong, and as quickly
correct himself. Judas moved deliberately to a decision, but
once convinced of it, refused to change. For he thought that de-
liberation could never reach a wrong conclusion or make a bad
choice–while convinced that haste often did both!

It wasn't because Judas held a political and Peter a spiritual
conviction about the Messiah. Every disciple sought a political

Messiah. History implanted that hope in Israel's national life, whether they looked in scripture, inter-testamental conflicts, wars, politics, divisions or Roman occupation. Exacerbated by subjection, tempered by delay and conditioned by habit, Israel wanted the conquered peoples' revenge on Rome and restoration to David's supremacy.

It wasn't even because Peter offered Jesus resolute and unreserved discipleship while Judas offered only tentative and conditional discipleship. We can't always extrapolate initial convictions about Jesus into final response to Jesus. Some who later became steadfast disciples began as provisional followers. Others who initially expressed interest ultimately withdrew from him.

How can we account for the Master's disproportionate evaluation of each man's sin? Perhaps because the *source* of their respective actions unerringly prescripted their ultimate outcome; one could be, the other couldn't be salvaged. Simon's abrupt denial came from an outside source preying on a mercurial disposition, while Judas' sin originated in his *motives.* In Gethsemane, hazarding his life, Peter courageously drew a sword to defend Jesus. In Caiphas' courtyard, safe from harm, a female's voice panicked him into denial! Judas, however, *on his own,* with malice aforethought deliberately plotted his way to betrayal. He reached that decision over an eighteen month period, despite evidence that Jesus was right; and retained the decision over the next twelve months, despite overwhelming evidence that Judas was wrong. As surely as Peter's instant of denial occurred in his impulsive nature, Judas' instant of betrayal occurred within his settled disposition. However hypocritical Simon's denial was, he never intended to deny. However sincere Judas' kiss in Gethsemane, he intentionally betrayed. What sprang from outside forces to discompose Simon identified only his emotional immaturity; what sprang from inner convictions to drive Judas identified his spiritual depravity.

Jesus foresaw that Peter's reckless misbehavior would be corrected by exposure, while Judas' premeditated treachery would be exacerbated by exposure; one would weep in shame, the other would grieve to suicide. In that sense, the external motivation in Peter's sin turned his grief *outward;* the inner resolution of Judas' sin turned his grief *inward*. Natural responses in each!

Judas would have been forgiven had he asked for it. Jesus returned an acre of mercy for every inch of repentance, but Judas refused that inch! Having deliberately arrived at his conclusion, he wouldn't renounce it—and could only rationalize it. It had all been mere *expedience* and, unfortunately hadn't succeeded. Since expedience sometimes fails—we propose and God disposes—no moral guilt should be accounted. It had been poor judgment, but if God condemned to Hell everyone guilty of poor judgement, who would be saved?

Naturally, his efforts to redress the wrong only increased his guilt. He returned the money, calling Jesus innocent blood; he remonstrated with the depraved leadership, cursing their hypocrisy; he lashed himself, condemning his treachery. But all attempts to make things right *with himself* failed because he battered himself with every blow except the one blow that would bring him to his knees–he had sinned against God and only God could remove the guilt!

His refusal to judge between wrong that God condemned and wrong that Judas rationalized finally overcame him in that lonely valley outside Jerusalem. When it did, he still couldn't face the fact that he had been guilty of catastrophic sin, not mere misjudgment. And he'll forever attribute injustice to God and innocence to himself because no one so sincere in his effort to establish the messianic kingdom should be so badly treated!

He'll admit mistakes in judgment. But that he had allowed himself to become a tool of Satan? Hardly! That he alone of all human beings would deserve the black sentence Jesus passed on him? Never! That Jesus, not he, is the tragic figure in the betrayal? Unthinkable!

Like the muddy Missouri entering the Mississippi, or the inky Rio Negro pouring its flood into the Amazon, Judas found his life increasingly discolored by his malformed opinions of God's kingdom, until his motives couldn't flow pure, having been corrupted and polluted by an unbowed, unbreakable political mind set!

Judas never heard a word to encourage his illusion, but his **craving** demanded its existence. Louder and louder it bellowed until Christ's very silence about the subject increased

Judas' need to hear it trumpeted! Until *whatever* spiritual thing Jesus said, Judas demanded it be a call to political activism and military conquest!

Like Aaron's rod before Pharaoh, that insistence devoured all the appeals Christ's teachings cast before him. He hung that hope around his neck like a snake charmer the serpent. And, in the end, fell strangled by it!

Judas and Peter went to separate destinies because they chose separate paths in life. Simon welcomed the kingdom of God, however Jesus defined it; Judas only if *he* defined it. Simon accepted Jesus, wherever it took him or whatever Jesus demanded he pay; Judas rejected Jesus *because* it took him where he refused to go and exacted costs he refused to pay.

EPILOGUE

Captivity to Babylon and Rome had created a national Jewish vision of suffering eclipsed by gratification; of captivity excelled by liberation. Personally scarred by his people's adversity, Judas focused backwards to both discover himself and define his future. By cross-breeding faith in Christ with his personal expectation of Messiah's work, Judas produced a hybrid Jesus wouldn't accept and couldn't be. However indefensible his position, and however clearly rejected by Jesus, Judas still demanded that Jesus subscribe to it, or pay the consequences!

But should God have repudiated his truth because Judas wanted to declare his deceit? Should Jesus overthrow God's sovereignty to reach a man whose demands would have grown stronger, tougher and more unreasonable as he was pacified, when the eleven accepted him as final authority? The certainty of God's presence in Christ saved them from the intimidation such mystery engendered in Judas! Belief in Jesus protected the eleven from Satan; belief in self exposed Judas to Satan.

Judas represents the result of doubt once welcomed, entertained and encouraged: a self pinballed from pole to pole, bounced out of control against the nearest obstacle, becoming a blistering mass of reservations and disputations; a spiritual chaos; the bitter nihilist; the acerbic satirist; the morbid cynic.

Judas broke with Jesus inwardly before he treacherously betrayed him. It would have been useless to talk him out of the deed without first talking him out of his broken faith! And Judas may have hated where his dark thoughts took him, but couldn't prevent them from dragging him there. Perhaps doubt ran out from him, hoping to sound on some far shore, echoing back assurance—but on and on it went unsounding, for no shore exists for doubt! Feeling suffocated by an ice-pack of unbelief, he may have sought an air-hole to once again breathe the oxygen of faith, but air-holes don't exist in skepticism!

For doubt lengthens like shadows and strengthens like prejudice! Doubt is like the Taipan's strike—hitting us repeatedly before we can react. It's like the sharpest needle, entering our lives so subtly it's unfelt, though not long before its injection saturates the soul!

Judas told the leaders he had betrayed "innocent blood." That was a strangely impersonal way to admit wrongdoing! Jesus could have been a ram or billy for those terms, since goats and lambs were *innocent*. Judas envisioned only a betrayed principle, not a betrayed person! *Innocent* may adequately describe the baby Jesus, but not the Christ he became. Innocence is a state of existence without choices. Righteousness, the state Jesus was in, is a state of existence achieved by making the right choices. His **perfect** righteousness resulted from his ability to make continually and infallibly right choices!

Innocent blood? Jesus? Never. His was an Overcomer's blood, the blood of one who met and conquered Satan and all his machinations and all the chaos his disordered mind miscreated!

However, Judas' admission of Christ's innocence certainly affected the Sanhedrin. For, at the trial before Pilate, they didn't produce the one person who would have been the state's most damaging witness if Jesus had been guilty of the crimes charged. Judas didn't appear! They didn't call him! With him the leaders could brashly strut before the governor, gloating, "We have a man whose personal experience can verify this rabbi's crimes." Then, sensationally, produce Judas himself. But no Judas appeared to vilify Christ. And that was because Judas reappeared before his former confederates and affirmed Christ's innocence! That rendered him a useless witness!

When Judas confessed his wrongdoing, the Sanhedrin replied, "What is that to us?", meaning they couldn't salve Judas' conscience. And neither could he! He could relate only to guilt, not relate guilt to its cause!

But some things never change. Somewhere in Hell today, where it's too dark for personal identification but light enough to distinguish figures, sitting apart is a man mumbling: "I didn't mean anything bad to happen to rabbi; and I did nothing to merit this Hell."

Those with him, impenitent of the sin that sent them there, have grown weary of hearing Judas' explanation and justification for his heinous deed. They may as well harden themselves, for Hell is full of those who never have and never will admit that God was right and they were wrong! Even in Hell, "ignominy thirsts" for the respect self-justification seeks but never finds!

Battles continue as soldiers die because the *army* they represent remains in the field. Like soldiers dying, Judas deserted his post, but another person occupied it, because an ongoing ministry outlasted a failed minister. Judas served as guide for those who arrested Jesus; Matthias would serve with those who preached Jesus. Judas bought a cemetery with his blood money; Matthias purchased souls with Christ's blood. Judas was one of their number, Peter said—affirming his role as a disciple. Judas hanged himself, Peter added—affirming his ultimate failure despite the privilege. Judas lived inside his limitations and died outside Christ's grace, but that didn't keep the apostles from losing their limitations inside Christ's potential. And if Judas quit believing because Jesus distressed him, they continued serving because Jesus gratified them. Like Judas, we can denounce the King for being a dictator—but others will submit to his rule. Like Judas, we can stay out of the kingdom, claiming the price of admission is too high—but others will pay it and inherit what we forfeit.